INSTANT V
THROUGH PREFI

INSTANT VOCABULARY
THROUGH PREFIXES
AND SUFFIXES

Timothy J. Vance

Kodansha International
Tokyo and New York

To Miriam

Distributed in the United States by Kodansha International/USA Ltd., 114 Fifth Avenue, New York, New York 10011. Published by Kodansha International Ltd., 17-14 Otowa 1-chome, Bunkyo-ku, Tokyo 112, and Kodansha International/USA. Copyright © 1990 by Kodansha International Ltd. All rights reserved.

First edition, 1990

Library of Congress Cataloging-in-Publication Data

Vance, Timothy J.
    Instant vocabulary through prefixes and suffixes / Timothy J. Vance. – 1st ed.
        p.   cm.   – (Power Japanese series)
    Includes bibliographical references.
    ISBN 4-7700-1500-3 : ¥1,000. – ISBN 0-87011-953-2 (U.S.) : $6.95
    1. Japanese language–Suffixes and prefixes. 2. Japanese language–Word formation. I. Title. II. Series.
PL561.V36 1991
495.6'82421–dc20   90-5015
                                        CIP

CONTENTS

PREFACE

The purpose of this book is to help intermediate students of Japanese develop proficiency in a narrow but important sector of vocabulary. All the elements I discuss have been borrowed into Japanese from Chinese, and in the uses I consider, they are like prefixes and suffixes. Teaching third- and fourth-year Japanese courses at the University of Hawaii has convinced me that students benefit from having their attention drawn to elements of this type. My feeling is that a relatively small investment of time can yield surprisingly large dividends in terms of improved reading ability.

Before moving on to the main text, I would like to touch briefly on a number of technical details and explain the linguistic terminology that occurs in the discussion. I have tried to avoid jargon as far as possible, but for the sake of conciseness, I have used a few terms that require some clarification.

Romanization and Accent

The romanization in this book is a version of the widely used Hepburn system and marks long vowels with macrons. For example, 空港 (airport) is romanized as *kūkō*. Standard accent patterns have been indicated by placing a corner (⌐) after the accented vowel: for example, 箸 (chopsticks) would be romanized as *hashi* and 天気 (weather) as *tenki*. In the case of a long vowel or a diphthong, traditional descriptions call for the corner to be placed after the first vowel: for example, 蚕 (silkworm) would be *kaiko* and 空気 (air) would be *kuuki*. In the case of 空気, however, since this book makes use of macrons instead of double vowels, *kuuki* would be romanized as *kūki*. It must be remembered, in such examples as this, that the accent falls after the first vowel, not after the second.

For reasons of economy, explicit marking of accent patterns in this book has been confined to the brief notations following the discussions of meaning and usage for each element. And even this notation is almost exclusively restricted to the part of the book devoted to suffix-like elements. The accent of words formed with prefix-like elements depends on the accent of the base, and is thus unpredictable. I have therefore not specified patterns for elements of this type. The only exception is 各- *kaku-* (q.v.), which is pronounced as an "accent phrase" of its own, separate from the base to which it is attached.

In contrast to prefix-like elements, the accent pattern of suffix-like elements is, with very few exceptions, predictable. For example, the pattern given for 者 *-sha* (q.v.) is ⌐*-sha*, indicating that the accented syllable of a word formed by adding *-sha* to a base will generally be the last syllable of the base, as in 容疑者 *yōgi-sha* (suspect). The pattern given for 家 *-ka* (q.v.) is "unaccented." This means that a word formed by adding *-ka* to a base will generally be unaccented, as in 小説家 *shōsetsu-ka* (novelist).

Prefixes and Suffixes

I mentioned above that the elements discussed in this book are used like prefixes and suffixes, but I avoided simply saying that they *are* prefixes and suffixes. For practical purposes, there is no need to worry about this terminological question, and I have not hesitated to use "prefixes and suffixes" in my title. Nonetheless, some readers may be interested in the technical question of what counts as a prefix or suffix, and a few simple examples will suffice to illustrate the basic problems involved.

One problem is that prefixes and suffixes are generally understood to be "bound" elements, that is, elements which can only occur as parts of words and not as words by themselves. For example, the English prefix "re-," as in "re-read," is bound in this sense; there is no independent word "re." Some of the Japanese elements considered in this book are in fact bound, but many are not. As an illustration, consider the element 一会 -*kai* (q.v.), which can be used as an independent word with the same meaning it has as a suffix-like element in words such as 運動会 *undō-kai* (sports meet). In many cases, it is difficult to decide whether or not an element is bound. One problematic example is the prefix-like element 非- *hi-* (q.v.), which expresses a kind of negation, as in 非金属 *hi-kinzoku* (nonmetal). There is also an independent word, 非 *hi* (a fault, a wrong), but the difference in meaning suggests that the two should not be considered the same element.

A second problem is that many of the suffix-like elements can combine with entire phrases in a way that is more typical of independent words than of suffixes. For example, in 毛沢東の影響下で *Mō Takutō no eikyō-ka de* (under the influence of Mao Zedong), 一下 *-ka* (q.v.) combines semantically with the entire phrase *Mō Takutō no eikyō* and not just with the word *eikyō*. Martin (1975: 90–138) calls elements that behave this way "quasi-restrictives" rather than suffixes.

A third problem is that prefix-like elements are sometimes pronounced as separate accent phrases, as noted above. The element 各- *kaku-* (q.v.) always behaves this way, but many other elements tend to be pronounced separately when added to relatively long bases—"base," here and throughout the main text, means the unit to which a prefix- or suffix-like element is attached. This sort of behavior is typical of independent words rather than parts of words. Martin (1975: 750–752) calls elements that behave this way "pseudo adnouns" rather than prefixes.

Etymology

It is convenient to divide the vocabulary of Japanese into three subsets on the basis of etymology. Both here and in the main text, I will use the label "native Japanese" for vocabulary elements (words or parts of words) that have been in use in Japanese since prehistoric times (i.e., 和語 *Wago*). I will say that elements borrowed from Chinese (i.e., 漢語 *Kango*) are of "Chinese origin," and that elements borrowed more recently from Western languages (i.e., 外来語 *gairai-go*) are "recent loanwords." As I noted above, all the elements treated in this book are of Chinese origin, and they typically combine with bases of Chinese origin, but many also combine freely with bases that are native Japanese words or recent loanwords.

Elements of Chinese origin play a role in the Japanese vocabulary that is similar in many respects to the role of Greek and Latin elements in the English vocabulary. The parallel is far from exact, but it is instructive if not pushed too far. The elements discussed in this book are reminiscent of English prefixes and suffixes of Greek or Latin origin, such as "anti-" (as in "anti-foreign"), "ex-" (as in "ex-husband"), "-ism" (as in "nationalism"), and "-ous" (as in "poisonous"). Like English words of Greek or Latin origin, Japanese words of Chinese origin tend to be bookish or technical, rather than colloquial, and to occur in sentences containing other words of the same type. As a broad generalization, it is fair to say that words formed with elements treated in this book are more likely to occur in newspaper articles, TV news broadcasts, scholarly writing, and somewhat elevated conversation than in everyday speech. I have tried to refrain from citing uncommon words or scientific terms as examples, but I have been unable to resist the temptation here and there. On the whole, an effort has been made to keep the Japanese sample sentences as simple as possible—that is, to minimize the number of *kanji* compounds and to avoid complex phrasing—so the student can devote his or her attention to the element to be learned. For consistency's sake, Japanese predicates have all been given in the non-formal form. The translations of elements in combination, as well as of the sample sentences, are often close to literal, in the hope that the student will be better able to grasp the structure of the Japanese.

10

Productivity

All the elements discussed in this book combine with bases "productively." In other words, it is possible to combine these elements with new bases and create novel words that are not listed in dictionaries. It is important to keep in mind, however, that productivity in this sense is a matter of degree. Some patterns of combination are more productive than others. There are also individual differences among speakers. Native speakers of Japanese often disagree with each other about the precise range of use of any given element. Individual native speakers may very well feel that some of the examples are "odd" or just plain "wrong." Readers should not feel too disconcerted at this state of affairs. Disagreements of this kind are a fact of life in every language.

All the elements discussed in this book combine with bases that are themselves independent words, but they are not in the language at large limited to combinations of this type. Consider the word 瞬発力 *shunpatsu-ryoku* (muscle power that can be put into action instantly), which can be analyzed as the element -力 *-ryoku* (q.v.) added to a base consisting of two elements of Chinese origin. This base is not an independent word; it occurs only in combination with *-ryoku*. I have excluded marginal examples of this kind from my discussion.

The elements treated in this book also occur in combination with single elements of Chinese origin. For example, the element -人 *-jin* (q.v.) occurs in 白人 *hakujin* (caucasian person), and although 白 *haku-* (white) is not an independent word, the combination is semantically parallel to words such as 東洋人 *tōyō-jin* (oriental person). Nonetheless, I have excluded two-element combinations like *hakujin* from my discussion because the contribution a given element makes in such examples is generally quite varied. Compare the word 殺人 *satsujin* (murder), which is clearly not parallel to *hakujin*.

Part of Speech

The words cited as examples in this book are all nouns, but this traditional part-of-speech label is not very informative, since there are several different kinds of nouns in Japanese. Interested readers should consult Martin (1975: 176–183) for a rigorous discussion of this problem. I use the term ''free noun'' to mean a word that can occur (1) followed by *ga*, *o*, etc. as a subject, direct object, etc.; (2) followed by *no* as a noun modifier; and (3) followed by a form of *da* as a predicate. Words like 船 *fune* (boat) and 今 *ima* (now) are free nouns. There are other words, such as 突然 *totsuzen* (sudden), which can occur as a noun modifier (followed by *no*) and as a predicate (followed by a form of *da*) but not as subjects, direct objects, etc. I consider words of this type nouns, but they are not free nouns, and when I cite them as examples, I add *no* in parentheses to the romanization: *totsuzen (no)*.

I use the term ''adjectival noun'' to mean a word that can occur (1) followed by *na* as a noun modifier and (2) followed by a form of *da* as a predicate. Words of this kind are known as *keiyō-dōshi* (形容動詞) in traditional Japanese grammar, and they are often called adjectives in textbooks. The word 静か *shizuka* (quiet) is a typical example, and when I cite an adjectival noun as an example, I add *na* in parentheses to the romanization: *shizuka (na)*. Some words can function either as free nouns or as adjectival nouns, One example is 自由 *jiyū* (freedom / free), and when I cite a word of this type as an example, I add / ~ *(na)* to the romanization: *jiyū / ~ (na)*.

Organization of the Text

I have chosen over sixty elements to treat at some length in the main text. My decisions about which items to include were not based on any explicit criteria. I simply chose the elements I felt were especially common or especially worthy of attention. Another writer would undoubtedly make somewhat different choices. Among these elements, I have given more examples for those that I think are particularly important. Obviously, the list is not exhaustive. I have tried to include only elements that seem likely to occur with some frequency in the kinds of reading material that intermediate students usually encounter. The sample sentences have been kept as simple as possible so that the student might concentrate his or her attention on the element to be learned.

For each element treated in the main text, I have included a brief discussion of meaning and use. I have tried to make these discussions informative, and many include references to works listed in the Bibliography, but the discussions are by no means rigorous linguistic analyses.

Acknowledgments

This book could not have been written without a great deal of help, and I would like to express my thanks here. Michael Brase and Suzuki Shigeyoshi of Kodansha International suggested the project to me in the first place and shepherded it through the publication process. Much of the material was gathered during the 1988–89 academic year when I was a research fellow at Rikkyō University in Tokyo. Kishiko Hayashi Vance read all the example sentences in the draft manuscript and suggested many improvements. Nobuko Ochner and Machiko Netsu provided thoughtful advice on a number of perplexing points. Haruko Cook took time out of her busy schedule to read and comment on the initial draft of the entire manuscript, and the finished product has benefited enormously from her careful scrutiny.

PREFIXES

超
CHŌ

Approximate English Equivalents:
super-, ultra-; supra-.

A word formed with *chō-* most commonly denotes an extreme degree or extreme example of what is denoted by the base (examples 1, 2, 3, 4). In other cases, however, a word formed with *chō-* means "transcending" what is denoted by the base (example 5).

(1) 超伝導 *chō-dendō* "superconduction."

BASE: 伝導 *dendō* "conduction."

超伝導が注目されるようになった。
Chō-dendō ga chūmoku sareru yō ni natta.
Superconduction has come to attract attention.

(2) 超デラックス *chō-derakkusu (na)* "superdeluxe."

BASE: デラックス *derakkusu (na)* "deluxe."

ハワイに超デラックスなホテルが建てられた。
Hawai ni chō-derakkusu na hoteru ga taterareta.
Superdeluxe hotels were built in Hawaii.

(3) 超満員 *chō-man'in (no)* "crowded beyond capacity."

BASE: 満員 *man'in (no)* "crowded to capacity."

彼女は毎朝、超満員の電車に乗る。
Kanojo wa maiasa, chō-man'in no densha ni noru.
Every morning she rides a train packed to overflowing.

(4) 超大国 *chō-taikoku* "superpower."

BASE: 大国 *taikoku* "powerful country."

世界の超大国といわれるのはソ連とアメリカだ。
Sekai no chō-taikoku to iwareru no wa Soren to Amerika da.
The countries said to be global superpowers are the Soviet Union
    and the United States.

(5) 超党派 *chō-tōha (no)* "nonpartisan."

BASE: 党派 *tōha* "faction, party."

超党派の委員会ができた。
Chō-tōha no iin-kai ga dekita.
A nonpartisan committee was formed.

一流 *ichiryū (no)* "first-rate."

超一流 *chō-ichiryū (no)*
  "ultra-first-rate."

国家主義 *kokka-shugi*
  "nationalism."

超国家主義 *chō-kokka-shugi*
  "ultra-nationalism."

スピード *supīdo* "speed."

超スピード *chō-supīdo*
  "super-speed."

能力 *nōryoku* "ability."

超能力 *chō-nōryoku*
  "supernatural power."

Approximate English Equivalent:
great.

DAI

The semantic effect of adding *dai-* to a base is similar to the effect in English of modifying a word with "great" or "greatly." The semantic range of *dai-* is roughly "large, serious, extreme, excellent, grand." With few exceptions, the base is a noun or a nominal adjective, and the word with *dai-* falls in the same category. The range of use of *dai-* overlaps with that of 名- *mei-* (not included), but *mei-* is added only to noun bases.

(1) 大反対 *dai-hantai* "strong opposition."

BASE: 反対 *hantai* "opposition."

母は娘の結婚に大反対だった。

Haha wa musume no kekkon ni dai-hantai datta.

The mother was strongly opposed to her daughter's marriage.

(2) 大ホームラン *dai-hōmuran* "long home run."

BASE: ホームラン *hōmuran* "home run."

田中選手は140メートル以上の大ホームランを打った。

Tanaka-senshu wa hyakuyonjū-mētoru ijō no dai-hōmuran o ut-ta.

Tanaka hit a tremendous home run of over 140 meters.

(3) 大洪水 *dai-kōzui* "great flood."

BASE: 洪水 *kōzui* "flood."

1933年の大洪水でたくさんの人が死んだ。

Senkyūhyaku-sanjūsan-nen no dai-kōzui de takusan no hito ga shinda.

Many people died in the great flood of 1933.

17

(4) 大流行 *dai-ryūkō* "great popularity."

BASE: 流行 *ryūkō* "popularity."

フラフープは日本でもアメリカでも大流行した。

Furafūpu wa Nihon de mo Amerika de mo dai-ryūkō shita.

The hula hoop was enormously popular both in Japan and in the
　　United States.

(5) 大作家 *dai-sakka* "great writer."

BASE: 作家 *sakka* "writer."

ディケンズは19世紀の大作家だった。

Dikenzu wa jūkyū-seiki no dai-sakka datta.

Dickens was a great writer of the 19th century.

豊作　　*hōsaku* "good harvest."　　　　恐慌　　*kyōkō* "panic."
大豊作　*dai-hōsaku*　　　　　　　　　大恐慌　*dai-kyōkō* "great panic."
　　　　"extremely good harvest."
　　　　　　　　　　　　　　　　　成功　　*seikō* "success."
敗北　　*haiboku* "defeat."　　　　　　大成功　*dai-seikō*
大敗北　*dai-haiboku*　　　　　　　　　　　　"great success."
　　　　"great defeat."

Approximate English Equivalents:
un-, non-, dis-.

FU

A word formed with *fu-* involves a negation of what is
denoted by the base. The base may be either a noun or an
adjectival noun, and when the base is a noun, the word
with *fu-* may be a noun (examples 4, 7) or, more commonly, an adjectival noun (examples 1, 2, 5, 6, 8). In some
cases, a word with *fu-* can function as either: 不景気 *fu-*
keiki / ～ *(na)* "(economic) depression / (economically)
depressed." In range of use, *fu-* overlaps with 非- *hi-*
(q.v.) and 無- *mu-* (q.v.); for details, see Aihara (1986)
and Martin (1975: 388–391, 763–765). Words with *fu-* tend
to involve an unfavorable evaluation (Zimmer 1964: 75),
and unlike *hi-* and *mu-*, *fu-* can mean "bad" (example 7).
There are a few words formed with etymologically related
不- *bu-* instead of *fu-*: 不躾 *bu-shitsuke (na)* (ill-mannered).

18

(1) 不安定 *fu-antei (na)* "unstable."

BASE: 安定 *antei* "stability."

漁業はとても不安定な職業だ。
Gyogyō wa totemo fu-antei na shokugyō da.
The fishing industry is a very unstable business.

(2) 不衛生 *fu-eisei (na)* "unsanitary."

BASE: 衛生 *eisei* "sanitation."

不衛生なので、そのレストランには行きたくない。
Fu-eisei na no de, sono resutoran ni wa ikitaku nai.
I don't want to go to that restaurant because it's unsanitary.

(3) 不必要 *fu-hitsuyō (na)* "unnecessary."

BASE: 必要 *hitsuyō* / ~ *(na)* "necessity / necessary."

彼の話はいつも不必要に細かい。
Kare no hanashi wa itsu mo fu-hitsuyō ni komakai.
What he says is always unnecessarily detailed.

(4) 不一致 *fu-itchi* "disagreement."

BASE: 一致 *itchi* "agreement."

意見の不一致を恐れてはいけない。
Iken no fu-itchi o osorete wa ikenai.
You should not fear differences of opinion.

(5) 不規則 *fu-kisoku (na)* "irregular."

BASE: 規則 *kisoku* "rule."

英語には不規則な動詞がたくさんある。
Eigo ni wa fu-kisoku na dōshi ga takusan aru.
In English there are many irregular verbs.

(6) 不慣れ *fu-nare (na)* "unaccustomed."

BASE: 慣れ *nare* "getting accustomed."

中国人の彼女は、まだ日本の生活に不慣れだ。
Chūgoku-jin no kanojo wa, mada Nihon no seikatsu ni fu-nare da.
A Chinese, she is still unaccustomed to Japanese life.

(7) 不成績 *fu-seiseki* "poor showing."

BASE: 成績 *seiseki* "showing, results."

日本チームは今回の試合も不成績に終わった。

Nihon-chīmu wa konkai no shiai mo fu-seiseki ni owatta.
The Japanese team made a poor showing in this match also.

(8) 不自然 *fu-shizen (na)* "unnatural."

BASE: 自然 *shizen* / ~ *(na)* "nature / natural."

不自然な言葉使いは避けるべきだ。
Fu-shizen na kotoba-zukai wa sakeru beki da.
Unnatural language should be avoided.

(9) 不適当 *fu-tekitō (na)* "inappropriate."

BASE: 適当 *tekitō (na)* "appropriate."

個人的な記事はこの雑誌に不適当だ。
Kojin-teki na kiji wa kono zasshi ni fu-tekitō da.
Articles of a personal nature are inappropriate to this magazine.

(10) 不透明 *fu-tōmei (na)* "opaque."

BASE: 透明 *tōmei (na)* "transparent."

新しい政策は国民には全く不透明だった。
Atarashii seisaku wa kokumin ni wa mattaku fu-tōmei datta.
The new political policy was completely opaque to the people.

合格　*gōkaku* "passing, success."　　可能　*kanō (na)* "possible."
不合格　*fu-gōkaku*　　　　　　　不可能　*fu-kanō (na)*
　　　"flunking, failure."　　　　　　　"impossible."

十分　*jūbun (na)* "sufficient."　　参加　*sanka* "participation."
不十分　*fu-jūbun (na)*　　　　　不参加　*fu-sanka*
　　　"insufficient."　　　　　　　　　"nonparticipation."

Approximate English Equivalents:
non-, un-.

A word formed with *hi-* involves a negation of what is
denoted by the base. In most cases, the base is a noun, but
hi- can also be added to adjectival nouns ending in -的
-teki (q.v.). When the base is a free noun, a word with *hi-*
may be a free noun (examples 1, 7), a non-free noun (examples 2, 3, 5, 9), or an adjectival noun (examples 4, 8). In
range of use, *hi-* overlaps with 不- *fu-* (q.v.) and 無- *mu-*

(q.v.), although only *hi-* can be added to bases ending with *-teki*. For details, see Aihara (1986) and Martin (1975: 388–391, 763–765). In contrast to words with *fu-*, words with *hi-* tend to involve a neutral rather than unfavorable evaluation.

(1) 非暴力 *hi-bōryoku* "non-violence."
BASE: 暴力 *bōryoku* "violence."
ガンジーやキングは非暴力を主張した。
Ganjī ya Kingu wa hi-bōryoku o shuchō shita.
Gandhi and King advocated non-violence.

(2) 非武装 *hi-busō (no)* "unarmed."
BASE: 武装 *busō* "armament."
国民は非武装中立をのぞんだ。
Kokumin wa hi-busō-chūritsu o nozonda.
The people hoped for unarmed neutrality.

(3) 非同盟 *hi-dōmei (no)* "non-aligned."
BASE: 同盟 *dōmei* "alliance."
スイスやスウェーデンは非同盟国だ。
Suisu ya Suēden wa hi-dōmei-koku da.
Switzerland and Sweden are non-aligned countries.

(4) 非常識 *hi-jōshiki (na)* "absurd."
BASE: 常識 *jōshiki* "common sense."
そんな非常識な計画は採用されるはずがない。
Sonna hi-jōshiki na keikaku wa saiyō sareru hazu ga nai.
Such an absurd plan will surely not be adopted.

(5) 非課税 *hi-kazei (no)* "tax-exempt."
BASE: 課税 *kazei* "taxation."
来年から薬は非課税になる。
Rainen kara kusuri wa hi-kazei ni naru.
Starting next year, medicine will be made tax-exempt.

(6) 非公式 *hi-kōshiki (no)* "unofficial."
BASE: 公式 *kōshiki (no)* "official."
彼の発言は非公式だった。
Kare no hatsugen wa hi-kōshiki datta.
His statement was unofficial.

(7) 非組合員 *hi-kumiai-in* "non-union member."

BASE: 組合員 *kumiai-in* "union member."

60人のうち51人が非組合員だ。
Rokujū-nin no uchi gojūichi-nin ga hi-kumiai-in da.
Of the 60, 51 are not members of the union.

(8) 非人情 *hi-ninjō (na)* "inhuman."

BASE: 人情 *ninjō* "human feelings."

このごろ非人情な行為が目立つ。
Konogoro hi-ninjō na kōi ga medatsu.
There are a lot of inhuman acts these days.

(9) 非オペック *hi-Opekku (no)* "non-OPEC."

BASE: オペック *Opekku* "OPEC."

非オペック産油国は値上げをしなかった。
Hi-Opekku-san'yukoku wa neage o shinakatta.
The non-OPEC oil-producing countries didn't raise their prices.

(10) 非生産的 *hi-seisan-teki* "unproductive."

BASE: 生産的 *seisan-teki* "productive."

社長は非生産的なシステムを改めるために努力した。
Shachō wa hi-seisan-teki na shisutemu o aratameru tame ni doryoku shita.
The company president made an effort to reform unproductive systems.

国民　*kokumin* "citizen."
非国民　*hi-kokumin* "unpatriotic person."

金属　*kinzoku* "metal."
非金属　*hi-kinzoku* "non-metal."

科学的　*kagaku-teki (na)* "scientific."
非科学的　*hi-kagaku-teki (na)* "unscientific."

合法　*gōhō (na)* "lawful, legal."
非合法　*hi-gōhō (na)* "unlawful, illegal."

各
KAKU

Approximate English Equivalents:
each, every.

A word formed with *kaku-* denotes each and every thing of the type specified by the base. Words with *kaku-* are often combined with a redundant ごとに *-goto ni* (to/for each; examples 2, 3). The range of *kaku-* overlaps with 全 *zen-* (q.v.), but unlike *zen-*, *kaku-* cannot be used to mean all of a single thing.

Accent: *kāku-*⌐.

(1) 各大臣 *kaku-daijin* "each minister."

BASE: 大臣 *daijin* "cabinet minister."

各大臣が演説をした。
Kaku-daijin ga enzetsu o shita.
Each minister gave a speech.

(2) 各段階 *kaku-dankai* "every stage."

BASE: 段階 *dankai* "stage."

工事の進行は各段階ごとに報告されていた。
Kōji no shinkō wa kaku-dankai goto ni hōkoku sarete ita.
The progress of the construction work was being reported at every stage.

(3) 各ジャンル *kaku-janru* "every genre."

BASE: ジャンル *janru* "genre."

この大学では，文学の各ジャンルごとに専門の教授がいる。
Kono daigaku de wa, bungaku no kaku-janru goto ni senmon no kyōju ga iru.
At this university, there are professors who specialize in every literary genre.

(4) 各家庭 *kaku-katei* "every household."

BASE: 家庭 *katei* "household."

今では各家庭にカラーテレビがある。
Ima de wa kaku-katei ni karā-terebi ga aru.
There is now a color television in every household.

(5) 各組合 *kaku-kumiai* "every union."

BASE: 組合 *kumiai* "union."

各組合は話し合いをくり返した。
Kaku-kumiai wa hanashi-ai o kurikaeshita.
The individual unions held repeated talks.

学校 *gakkō* "school."
各学校 *kaku-gakkō*
    "each school."

部門 *bumon*
    "department, branch, field."
各部門 *kaku-bumon*
    "each department."

方面 *hōmen* "direction, field."
各方面 *kaku-hōmen*
    "each direction, field."

クラス *kurasu* "class."
各クラス *kaku-kurasu*
    "each class."

旧
KYŪ

Approximate English Equivalents:
old, former, ex-.

The meaning of *kyū-* is "old, old-fashioned" (examples 3, 4) or "former" (examples 1, 5). In some cases, the two meanings are hard to distinguish (example 2). The range of use of 前- *zen-* "former" (not included) overlaps with that of *kyū-*. The antonym of *kyū-* is 新- *shin-* (q.v.).

(1) 旧所有者 *kyū-shoyū-sha* "former owner."

BASE: 所有者 *shoyū-sha* "owner."

私はこの車の旧所有者に会った。
Watashi wa kono kuruma no kyū-shoyū-sha ni atta.
I met the former owner of this car.

(2) 旧仮名遣い *kyū-kana-zukai* "old kana spelling."

BASE: 仮名遣い *kana-zukai* "kana spelling."

旧仮名遣いでは,「大水」は「おほみづ」と書く。
Kyū-kana-zukai de wa, "ōmizu" wa "o-ho-mi-dzu" to kaku.
In old kana spelling, "ōmizu" is written as "o-ho-mi-dzu."

(3) 旧世代 *kyū-sedai* "the old generation."

BASE: 世代 *sedai* "generation."

あの老人は旧世代の唯一の生き残りだ。
Ano rōjin wa kyū-sedai no yuiitsu no ikinokori da.
That old fellow is the sole survivor of the old generation.

(4) 旧思想 *kyū-shisō* "outmoded ideas."

BASE: 思想 *shisō* "ideas."

彼は旧思想の持ち主だ。
Kare wa kyū-shisō no mochi-nushi da.
His ideas are outmoded.

(5) 旧敵国 *kyū-tekikoku* "former enemy nation."

BASE: 敵国 *tekikoku* "enemy nation."

今では旧敵国へ旅行に出かける若者もいる。
Ima de wa kyū-tekikoku e ryokō ni dekakeru wakamono mo iru.
Young people now go off on trips to former enemy nations.

秩序 *chitsujo* "orderliness, social order."	植民地 *shokumin-chi* "colony."
旧秩序 *kyū-chitsujo* "the old order."	旧植民地 *kyū-shokumin-chi* "former colony."
工場 *kōjō* "factory."	制度 *seido* "system, organization."
旧工場 *kyū-kōjō* "the old factory."	旧制度 *kyū-seido* "the old system."

未
MI

Approximate English Equivalents:
not yet, un-.

A word formed with *mi-* functions as a noun modifier when followed by *no* (examples 1, 3, 5) and as a predicate when followed by a form of *da* (examples 2, 4). In most cases, the base denotes an action, and the word with *mi-* denotes the attribute of not yet having been affected by that action. The word 未成年 *mi-seinen (no)* (not yet legal age) is exceptional in having a base that does not denote an action. It is the implication of future change that clearly distinguishes *mi-* from 不- *fu-* (q.v.), *hi-* (q.v.), and *mu-* (q.v.). For example, compare 未確定 *mi-kakutei (no)* (not yet determined) with 不確定 *fu-kakutei (no)* (indeterminate).

(1) 未分析 *mi-bunseki (no)* "not yet analyzed."

BASE: 分析 *bunseki* "analysis."

発掘された金属は未分析のままになっている。
Hakkutsu sareta kinzoku wa mi-bunseki no mama ni natte iru.
The excavated metal remains unanalyzed.

(2) 未発見 *mi-hakken (no)* "not yet discovered."

BASE: 発見 *hakken* "discovery."

この病気に利く薬は未発見だ。
Kono byōki ni kiku kusuri wa mi-hakken da.
The medicine that will cure this disease has yet to be discovered.

(3) 未解決 *mi-kaiketsu (no)* "not yet solved."

BASE: 解決 *kaiketsu* "solution."

基本問題すら未解決のままだ。
Kihon-mondai sura mi-kaiketsu no mama da.
Even the basic problems remain unresolved.

(4) 未公認 *mi-kōnin (no)* "not yet official."

BASE: 公認 *kōnin* "official recognition."

未公認だが世界記録を出した。
Mi-kōnin da ga sekai-kiroku o dashita.
It's still pending, but he broke the world record.

(5) 未経験 *mi-keiken (no)* "not yet experienced."

BASE: 経験 *keiken* "experience."

彼女の前には未経験の仕事が山ほどあった。
Kanojo no mae ni wa mi-keiken no shigoto ga yama-hodo atta.
She was faced by a mountain of work that she had never done
  before.

発表 *happyō*
    "announcement, release."
未発表 *mi-happyō (no)*
    "unannounced."

発達 *hattatsu* "development."
未発達 *mi-hattatsu (na / no)*
    "not yet developed."

完成 *kansei* "completion."
未完成 *mi-kansei (no)*
    "not yet completed."

公開 *kōkai* "making public."
未公開 *mi-kōkai (no)*
    "not yet made public."

無
MU

Approximate English Equivalents:
un-, -less.

A word formed with *mu-* means "lacking" what is denoted by the base and can usually be paraphrased with −な し -*nashi*. For example, 無利息 *mu-risoku (no)* (interest-free) is virtually synonymous with 利息なし *risoku-nashi (no)* (without interest). In range of use, *mu-* overlaps to some extent with 不− *fu-* (q.v.) and 非− *hi-* (q.v.), but *mu-* differs in requiring a free noun as a base (Martin 1975: 390). Words with *mu-* can function as adverbs when followed by *ni* (example 3) or *de* (examples 1, 10) and as predicates when followed by a form of *da* (examples 5, 6). They can also function as noun modifiers (examples 2, 7, 8, 9). Some words with *mu-* are adjectival nouns and take *na* before a noun (examples 2, 6), whereas others require *no* (examples 1, 4, 7, 8, 9, 10); still others can take either *na* or *no* (examples 3, 5). There are a few words formed with etymologically related 無− *bu-* instead of *mu-*: 無用心 *bu-yōjin (na)* (unsafe).

(1) 無着陸 *mu-chakuriku (no)* "nonstop."

BASE: 着陸 *chakuriku* "landing."

アメリカなら、東京から無着陸で行ける。
Amerika nara, Tōkyō kara mu-chakuriku de ikeru.
If the United States (is the destination), you can go nonstop from Tokyo.

(2) 無意味 *mu-imi (na)* "meaningless."

BASE: 意味 *imi* "meaning."

政治家の演説はたいてい無意味なおしゃべりに過ぎない。
Seiji-ka no enzetsu wa taitei mu-imi na oshaberi ni suginai.
Politicians' speeches are usually just meaningless chatter.

(3) 無意識 *mu-ishiki (na / no)* "unconscious."

BASE: 意識 *ishiki* "consciousness."

少しでも練習すれば無意識にできるようになる。
Sukoshi de mo renshū sureba mu-ishiki ni dekiru yō ni naru.

If you practice just a little, you become able to do it unconsciously.

(4) 無条件 *mu-jōken (no)* "unconditional."

BASE: 条件 *jōken* "condition."

連合国は日本に無条件降伏を要求した。
Rengō-koku wa Nihon ni mu-jōken-kōfuku o yōkyū shita.
The Allied Powers demanded that Japan surrender unconditionally.

(5) 無関係 *mu-kankei (na / no)* "unconnected, irrelevant."

BASE: 関係 *kankei* "connection."

国籍や人種は頭と無関係だ。
Kokuseki ya jinshu wa atama to mu-kankei da.
Nationality and race are irrelevant to intellect.

(6) 無計画 *mu-keikaku (na)* "unplanned."

BASE: 計画 *keikaku* "plan."

彼のやり方はいつでも無計画だった。
Kare no yarikata wa itsu de mo mu-keikaku datta.
The way he did things was always unplanned.

(7) 無試験 *mu-shiken (no)* "without exams."

BASE: 試験 *shiken* "exam."

無試験の学校も作るべきだ。
Mu-shiken no gakkō mo tsukuru beki da.
Schools that don't have exams should also be created.

(8) 無届け *mu-todoke (no)* "without notification."

BASE: 届け *todoke* "notification."

労働組合は無届けの集会を開いた。
Rōdō-kumiai wa mu-todoke no shūkai o hiraita.
The union held a meeting without notifying the authorities.

(9) 無得点 *mu-tokuten (no)* "scoreless."

BASE: 得点 *tokuten* "points scored."

試合は無得点のまま引き分けに終わった。
Shiai wa mu-tokuten no mama hikiwake ni owatta.
The game remained scoreless and ended in a tie.

(10) 無投票 *mu-tōhyō (no)* "without a vote."

BASE: 投票 *tōhyō* "voting."

知事は無投票で再選された。
Chiji wa mu-tōhyō de saisen sareta.
The govenor was reelected without a vote.

秩序 *chitsujo* "order, system."
無秩序 *mu-chitsujo (na)* "disorganized, unsystematic."

免許 *menkyo* "license."
無免許 *mu-menkyo (no)* "unlicensed."

制限 *seigen* "limit."
無制限 *mu-seigen (na/no)* "unlimited."

関心 *kanshin* "concern."
無関心 *mu-kanshin (na)* "indifference."

再
SAI

Approximate English Equivalents:
re-, repeat.

A word formed with *sai-* denotes a repetition of an action or activity denoted by the base.

(1) 再調査 *sai-chōsa* "repeat investigation."

BASE: 調査 *chōsa* "investigation."

新しい傾向を調べるため、1989年に再調査が行われた。
Atarashii keikō o shiraberu tame, senkyūhyaku-hachijūkyū-nen ni sai-chōsa ga okonawareta.
To check on new trends, a repeat investigation was carried out in 1989.

(2) 再放送 *sai-hōsō* "rebroadcast."

BASE: 放送 *hōsō* "broadcast."

あの人気ドラマはいつか再放送されるにちがいない。
Ano ninki-dorama wa itsu ka sai-hōsō sareru ni chigai nai.
That popular drama will certainly be rebroadcast sometime.

(3) 再スタート *sai-sutāto* "new start."

BASE: スタート *sutāto* "start."

山田さんは新しい職場で再スタートを切った。
Yamada-san wa atarashii shokuba de sai-sutāto o kitta.
Yamada made a fresh start at his new place of work.

(4) 再統一 *sai-tōitsu* "reunification."

BASE: 統一 *tōitsu* "unification."

東西ドイツの再統一は世界にいろいろな影響を及ぼすだろう。

Tōzai-Doitsu no sai-tōitsu wa sekai ni iroiro na eikyō o oyobosu darō.

The reunification of East and West Germany will have a variety of ramifications throughout the world.

(5) 再打ち上げ *sai-uchiage* "relaunch."

BASE: 打ち上げ *uchiage* "launch."

スペースシャトルの再打ち上げが決まった。

Supēsu-shatoru no sai-uchiage ga kimatta.

It was decided to relaunch the space shuttle.

軍備	*gunbi* "armaments."	開発	*kaihatsu* "development."
再軍備	*sai-gunbi* "rearmament."	再開発	*sai-kaihatsu* "redevelopment."
発見	*hakken* "discovery."		
再発見	*sai-hakken* "rediscovery."	投票	*tōhyō* "voting."
		再投票	*sai-tōhyō* "revoting."

新 SHIN

Approximate English Equivalent: new.

The semantic range of *shin-*, which is added to noun bases, is roughly the same as that of "new." In addition, *shin-* is the usual equivalent of *neo-* in words like 新古典主義 *shin-koten-shugi* (neo-classicism). The antonym of *shin-* is 旧– *kyū-* (q.v.).

(1) 新時代 *shin-jidai* "new era."

BASE: 時代 *jidai* "era."

戦後日本は新時代に入った。

Sengo Nihon wa shin-jidai ni haitta.

Japan entered a new era after the war.

(2) 新記録 *shin-kiroku* "new record."

BASE: 記録 *kiroku* "record."

中国の選手がマラソンで新記録を作った。

Chūgoku no senshu ga marason de shin-kiroku o tsukutta.

A Chinese athlete set a new record in the marathon.

(3) 新憲法 *shin-kenpō* "new constitution."

BASE: 憲法 *kenpō* "constitution."

新憲法と旧憲法では大きな違いがある。

Shin-kenpō to kyū-kenpō de wa ōki na chigai ga aru.

There is a big difference between the new and old constitutions.

(4) 新政権 *shin-seiken* "new regime."

BASE: 政権 *seiken* "regime."

新政権はまだうまくいっていない。

Shin-seiken wa mada umaku itte inai.

The new regime is not doing well yet.

(5) 新エネルギー *shin-enerugī* "new energy."

BASE: エネルギー *enerugī* "energy."

「新エネルギー」とは、エネルギーとして使われる太陽光や風力のことだ。

"Shin-enerugī" to wa, enerugī toshite tsukawareru taiyō-kō ya fūryoku no koto da.

"New energy" means sunlight, wind power, and such used as energy.

貿易法　*bōeki-hō* "trade law."		市長　*shichō* "mayor."
新貿易法　*shin-bōeki-hō* "new trade law."		新市長　*shin-shichō* "new mayor."
学年　*gakunen* "school year."		体制　*taisei* "system, regime."
新学年　*shin-gakunen* "new school year."		新体制　*shin-taisei* "new system, regime."

諸
SHO

Approximate English Equivalents:
several, various.

The essential function of *sho-* is to mark a noun base explicitly as plural (see Martin 1975: 151). In many cases, the English equivalents given above are too specific to be appropriate translations.

(1) 諸言語 *sho-gengo* "languages."

BASE: 言語 *gengo* "language."

彼はアジアの諸言語を研究している。

Kare wa Ajia no sho-gengo o kenkyū shite iru.

He is doing research on Asian languages.

(2) 諸活動 *sho-katsudō* "activities."

BASE: 活動 *katsudō* "activity."

暴力団の諸活動が大きな問題となってきた。

Bōryoku-dan no sho-katsudō ga ōki na mondai to natte kita.

The activities of criminal organizations have become a major problem.

(3) 諸機能 *sho-kinō* "functions."

BASE: 機能 *kinō* "function."

ワープロの諸機能は画面に現れる。

Wāpuro no sho-kinō wa gamen ni arawareru.

A word processor's functions appear on the screen.

(4) 諸理由 *sho-riyū* "reasons."

BASE: 理由 *riyū* "reason."

「貿易摩擦の諸理由」というテーマが決まった。

"Bōeki-masatsu no sho-riyū" to iu tēma ga kimatta.

It was decided that the theme would be "Reasons for Trade Friction."

(5) 諸問題 *sho-mondai* "various problems."

BASE: 問題 *mondai* "problem."

その2国の間には未解決の諸問題がたくさんある。

Sono ni-koku no aida ni wa mi-kaiketsu no sho-mondai ga takusan aru.

There are still various unresolved problems between those two countries.

外国 *gaikoku* "foreign country."	費用 *hiyō* "expense, cost."
諸外国 *sho-gaikoku* "foreign countries."	諸費用 *sho-hiyō* "expenses."
制度 *seido* "system."	団体 *dantai* "group, party, body."
諸制度 *sho-seido* "systems."	諸団体 *sho-dantai* "groups."

総
SŌ

Approximate English Equivalents:
complete, total, general.

The meaning of *sō-* is roughly "all-encompassing." Typical bases include words denoting quantities (example 1), actions or activities (examples 2, 5), or persons in charge (example 3), although these are not the only possibilities.

(1) 総台数 *sō-daisū* "total number."

BASE: 台数 *daisū* "number (of vehicles)."

トラックの総台数は1000台を上回った。
Torakku no sō-daisū wa sen-dai o uwamawatta.
The total number of trucks went over 1,000.

(2) 総辞職 *sō-jishoku* "general resignation."

BASE: 辞職 *jishoku* "resignation."

内閣総辞職のうわさが立っている。
Naikaku sō-jishoku no uwasa ga tatte iru.
There is a rumor of a general resignation of the cabinet.

(3) 総監督 *sō-kantoku* "general director."

BASE: 監督 *kantoku* "foreman, manager, director."

安田氏は映画会社の総監督になった。
Yasuda-shi wa eiga-gaisha no sō-kantoku ni natta.
Mr. Yasuda became the general director of a movie company.

(4) 総索引 *sō-sakuin* "general index."

BASE: 索引 *sakuin* "index."

百科事典には総索引が必ず付いている。
Hyakka-jiten ni wa sō-sakuin ga kanarazu tsuite iru.
A general index is always included in an encyclopedia.

(5) 総崩れ *sō-kuzure* "total defeat."

BASE: 崩れ *kuzure* "defeat."

シード選手は総崩れになった。
Shīdo-senshu wa sō-kuzure ni natta.
All the seeded players lost.

人口 *jinkō* "population." 選挙 *senkyo* "election."
総人口 *sō-jinkō* 総選挙 *sō-senkyo*
　　 "total population." 　　 "general election."

面積 *menseki* "area." 売り上げ *uriage* "sales."
総面積 *sō-menseki* "total area." 総売り上げ *sō-uriage*
　　 "total sales."

Approximate English Equivalents:
all, whole.

A word formed with *zen-* denotes either all things (examples 1, 4) or one whole thing (examples 2, 3, 5) of the type specified by the base.

(1) 全分野 *zen-bun'ya* "all fields."

BASE: 分野 *bun'ya* "field."

この大学には、全分野にいい先生がいる。
Kono daigaku ni wa, zen-bun'ya ni ii sensei ga iru.
This university has good teachers in all fields.

(2) 全チーム *zen-chīmu* "whole team."

BASE: チーム *chīmu* "team."

オーナーは全チームを集めてパーティーをした。
Ōnā wa zen-chīmu o atsumete pātī o shita.
The owner got the whole team together and had a party.

(3) 全人生 *zen-jinsei* "whole life."

BASE: 人生 *jinsei* "life."

彼女は研究に全人生をかけてきた。
Kanojo wa kenkyū ni zen-jinsei o kakete kita.
She has devoted her whole life to research.

(4) 全家屋 *zen-kaoku* "all houses."

BASE: 家屋 *kaoku* "house."

台風によって全家屋の6割の屋根が飛んだ。
Taifū ni yotte zen-kaoku no roku-wari no yane ga tonda.
The roofs of 60% of all the houses were blown away by the typhoon.

(5) 全財産 *zen-zaisan* "whole fortune."

BASE: 財産 *zaisan* "fortune."

息子は全財産を6ヵ月でなくしてしまった。
Musuko wa zen-zaisan o rokkagetsu de nakushite shimatta.
The son lost his entire fortune in six months.

ページ *pēji* "page."

全ページ *zen-pēji*
　　"the full page, all pages."

人類 *jinrui* "humankind."

全人類 *zen-jinrui*
　　"all humanity."

世界 *sekai* "the world."

全世界 *zen-sekai*
　　"the whole world."

速力 *sokuryoku* "speed."

全速力 *zen-sokuryoku*
　　"full speed."

SUFFIXES

BETSU

Approximate English Equivalents:
classified by, according to.

A word formed with *-betsu* means "classified according to" the criterion denoted by the base. Words with *-betsu* are generally used as noun modifiers (either directly preceding the noun or with an intervening *no*, as in examples 2, 3, respectively), or are followed by *ni* and used adverbially (examples 1, 4, 5).

Accent: unaccented.

(1) 地域別 *chiiki-betsu (no)* "by region."

BASE: 地域 *chiiki* "region."

人口は下の図で地域別に示されている。
Jinkō wa shita no zu de chiiki-betsu ni shimesarete iru.
Population is shown by region in the figure below.

(2) 科目別 *kamoku-betsu (no)* "by subject."

BASE: 科目 *kamoku* "subject."

先生は科目別の得点を調べた。
Sensei wa kamoku-betsu no tokuten o shirabeta.
The teacher checked the scores subject by subject.

(3) 国家別 *kokka-betsu (no)* "by country."

BASE: 国家 *kokka* "country, nation, state."

車の国家別輸入額では日本が一番だ。
Kuruma no kokka-betsu yunyū-gaku de wa Nihon ga ichiban da.
In amount of car imports by country, Japan is number one.

(4) 目的別 *mokuteki-betsu (no)* "according to purpose."

BASE: 目的 *mokuteki* "purpose."

外国語の教科書は目的別に並んでいる。
Gaikoku-go no kyōkasho wa mokuteki-betsu ni narande iru.
The foreign-language textbooks are arranged according to purpose.

(5) 政党別 *seitō-betsu (no)* "by party."

BASE: 政党 *seitō* "political party."

政党別にパーティーが行われた。
Seitō-betsu ni pātī ga okonawareta.
Parties were held according to party affiliation.

ジャンル　*janru* "genre."
ジャンル別　*janru-betsu (no)*
　　　"by genre."

職業　*shokugyō* "occupation."
職業別　*shokugyō-betsu (no)*
　　　"by occupation."

国籍　*kokuseki* "nationality."
国籍別　*kokuseki-betsu (no)*
　　　"by nationality."

年齢　*nenrei* "age."
年齢別　*nenrei-betsu (no)*
　　　"by age."

部
BU

Approximate English Equivalents:
part; department; club, team.

A word formed with -*bu* denotes a part of some larger entity. It is typically a part of a place or thing (examples 1, 3), a department or division of an organization (examples 2, 4), or a club or team at a school or company (example 5). In the Japanese government, a department with a name ending in -*bu* is a subdivision of a larger unit with a name ending in 一庁 -*chō* (not included) or 一局 -*kyoku* (not included).

Accent: ˥-*bu*.

(1) 沿岸部 *engan-bu* "coastal area, littoral."

BASE: 沿岸 *engan* "coast, shore."

北アフリカの人口は沿岸部に集中している。
Kita-Afurika no jinkō wa engan-bu ni shūchū shite iru.
The population of North Africa is concentrated along the coast.

(2) 行政部 *gyōsei-bu* "executive branch."

BASE: 行政 *gyōsei* "administration."

アメリカの大統領は政府の行政部の第一人者だ。
Amerika no daitōryō wa seifu no gyōsei-bu no daiichinin-sha da.
The American president is the head of the executive branch of
　government.

(3) 下線部 *kasen-bu* "underlined part."

BASE: 下線 *kasen* "underline."

その文書の下線部に注意しよう。
Sono bunsho no kasen-bu ni chūi shiyō.
Let's take a good look at the underlined part of the text.

(4) 宣伝部 *senden-bu* "publicity department."

BASE: 宣伝 *senden* "publicity."

宣伝部の意見で、新聞に広告を出した。
Senden-bu no iken de, shinbun ni kōkoku o dashita.
Following the advice of the publicity department, an ad was placed in the newspaper.

(5) テニス部 *tenisu-bu* "tennis team (club)."

BASE: テニス *tenisu* "tennis."

テニス部に入らないと、学校のコートは使えない。
Tenisu-bu ni hairanai to, gakkō no kōto wa tsukaenai.
Unless you join the tennis team (club), you can't use the school courts.

中心 *chūshin* "center."
中心部 *chūshin-bu* "central part."

写真 *shashin* "photograph."
写真部 *shashin-bu* "photography club, department."

食品 *shokuhin* "food, groceries."
食品部 *shokuhin-bu* "food department."

編集 *henshū* "editing."
編集部 *henshū-bu* "editorial department."

BUTSU

Approximate English Equivalents: thing, substance.

A word formed with *-butsu* denotes an object or substance of a type specified by the base. In range of use, *-butsu* overlaps with several more specific elements, including 一液 *-eki* (not included), 一品 *-hin* (q.v.), 一質 *-shitsu* (not included), and 一体 *-tai* (not included).

Accent: ⁻*-butsu*.

(1) 爆発物 *bakuhatsu-butsu* "an explosive."

BASE: 爆発 *bakuhatsu* "explosion."

飛行機のなかで爆発物が見つかった。
Hikōki no naka de bakuhatsu-butsu ga mitsukatta.
Explosives were found in the airplane.

(2) 建築物 *kenchiku-butsu* "a structure, a building."

BASE: 建築 *kenchiku* "construction, architecture."

東京では古い建築物が少なくなっている。
Tōkyō de wa furui kenchiku-butsu ga sukunaku natte iru.
Old buildings have grown scarce in Tokyo.

(3) 廃棄物 *haiki-butsu* "waste product."

BASE: 廃棄 *haiki* "disposal, doing away with."

この川は廃棄物で汚くなってきた。
Kono kawa wa haiki-butsu de kitanaku natte kita.
This river has grown filthy with waste products.

(4) 印刷物 *insatsu-butsu* "printed matter."

BASE: 印刷 *insatsu* "printing."

印刷物の郵便料金は安い。
Insatsu-butsu no yūbin-ryōkin wa yasui.
Postage for printed matter is cheap.

(5) 化合物 *kagō-butsu* "compound."

BASE: 化合 *kagō* "chemical combination."

水は化合物で、元素ではない。
Mizu wa kagō-butsu de, genso de wa nai.
Water is a compound, not an element.

海産 *kaisan*
　　"marine production."
海産物 *kaisan-butsu*
　　"marine products."

流動 *ryūdō* "flowing."
流動物 *ryūdō-butsu*
　　"fluid substance."

出版 *shuppan* "publishing."
出版物 *shuppan-butsu*
　　"a publication."

郵便 *yūbin*
　　"postal service, mail."
郵便物 *yūbin-butsu*
　　"postal item, mail."

病
BYŌ

Approximate English Equivalents:
disease, illness.

A word formed with -*byō* denotes an illness that is specified in some way by the base. The base may be related to the illness in a wide variety of ways. Some of the possibilities are: the name of a researcher (example 1), the cause (example 2), the susceptible segment of the population (example 3), the symptoms (example 4), and the affected part of the body (example 5). The range of use of -*byō* overlaps with that of 一症 -*shō* (not included), although -*shō* has a more scientific ring.

Accent: unaccented.

(1) ハンセン病 *Hansen-byō* "Hansen's disease."

BASE: ハンセン *Hansen* "Hansen."

彼女はハンセン病にかかった。
Kanojo wa Hansen-byō ni kakatta.
She has come down with Hansen's disease.

(2) 公害病 *kōgai-byō* "illness caused by pollution."

BASE: 公害 *kōgai* "pollution."

住民は公害病を恐れていた。
Jūmin wa kōgai-byō o osorete ita.
The residents were afraid of pollution-related diseases.

(3) 老人病 *rōjin-byō* "geriatric disease."

BASE: 老人 *rōjin* "elderly person."

老人病の専門医がもっと必要だ。
Rōjin-byō no senmon-i ga motto hitsuyō da.
There is a need for more doctors specializing in geriatric diseases.

(4) ゴルフ病 *gorufu-byō* "golf-itis."

BASE: ゴルフ *gorufu* "golf."

田中さんはいろいろな人から「ゴルフ病」とか「ゴルフ気違い」とか呼ばれている。
Tanaka-san wa iroiro na hito kara "gorufu-byō" to ka "gorufu kichigai" to ka yobarete iru.

42

There are many people who say that Tanaka is "golf crazy" or has "golf-itis."

(5) 心臓病 *shinzō-byō* "heart disease."

BASE: 心臓 *shinzō* "heart."

戦後の日本では心臓病にかかる人が多くなってきた。
Sengo no Nihon de wa shinzō-byō ni kakaru hito ga ōku natte kita.

In postwar Japan, more people are coming down with heart diseases.

婦人 *fujin* "woman."
婦人病 *fujin-byō* "female disorder."

精神 *seishin* "mind."
精神病 *seishin-byō* "mental illness."

原爆 *genbaku* "atomic bomb."
原爆病 *genbaku-byō* "illness caused by atomic bomb."

職業 *shokugyō* "occupation."
職業病 *shokugyō-byō* "occupational disease."

調
CHŌ

Approximate English Equivalents: style, character.

A word formed with *-chō* denotes a style or character typical of what is denoted by the base. According to Bunka-chō (1975: 614), *-chō* is a near synonym of 一風 *-fū* (q.v.), but *-chō* is especially common with bases that denote something musical (example 5) or something linguistic (examples 3, 4). Grammatically, words with *-chō* are free nouns, whereas words with *-fū* are not.

Accent: unaccented.

(1) ビクトリア調 *Bikutoria-chō* "Victorian style."

BASE: ビクトリア *Bikutoria* "(Queen) Victoria"

ビクトリア調の大邸宅が遠くに見える。
Bikutoria-chō no dai-teitaku ga tōku ni mieru.
A Victorian-style mansion is seen in the distance.

(2) 軍服調 *gunpuku-chō* "military uniform style."

BASE: 軍服 *gunpuku* "military uniform."

43

政府が決めた服は軍服調だった。
Seifu ga kimeta fuku wa gunpuku-chō datta.
The clothing the government decided on is in the military-uniform style.

(3) 翻訳調 *hon'yaku-chō* "translation flavor."

BASE: 翻訳 *hon'yaku* "translation."

海外のニュースはときどき翻訳調になる。
Kaigai no nyūsu wa tokidoki hon'yaku-chō ni naru.
Foreign news sometimes sounds like translationese.

(4) 講義調 *kōgi-chō* "lecture style."

BASE: 講義 *kōgi* "lecture."

山本教授はどこでも講義調の話し方をする。
Yamamoto-kyōju wa doko de mo kōgi-chō no hanashikata o suru.
No matter where he is, Professor Yamamoto speaks as if he's giving a lecture.

(5) 民謡調 *min'yō-chō* "folk-song style."

BASE: 民謡 *min'yō* "folk song."

最近、流行歌はだんだん民謡調ではなくなっている。
Saikin, ryūkō-ka wa dandan min'yō-chō de wa naku natte iru.
Recently, popular songs have gradually lost their folk-song flavor.

美文 *bibun* "flowery prose."	講談 *kōdan* "narrative."
美文調 *bibun-chō* "flowery style."	講談調 *kōdan-chō* "narrative style."
復古 *fukko* "revival."	口語 *kōgo* "colloquial language."
復古調 *fukko-chō* "reactionary character."	口語調 *kōgo-chō* "colloquial style."

Approximate English Equivalents:
during, in the midst of.

A word formed with *-chū* can mean "during" or "while" what is denoted by the base (examples 2, 7, 8). This is the only possibility when the base denotes a period of time (ex-

44

ample 7), and in this meaning -*chū* can be paraphrased as
の間 *no aida*. A word formed with -*chū* can also mean "in
the midst of" what is denoted by the base (examples 1, 3,
4, 5, 6, 9, 10), and in this meaning -*chū* can usually be
paraphrased as して/されている最中 *shite / sarete iru*
saichū. When no particle follows, a word with -*chū* functions as an adverb (examples 2, 10). It functions as a time
noun when followed by *ni* (examples 7, 8), as a noun
modifier when followed by *no* (examples 1, 6), and as a
predicate when followed by だ *da* etc. (examples 3, 4, 9).
For details, see Martin (1975: 881–883). There are also
words in which -*chū* follows a base that cannot be construed as a state, activity, or time span. In such cases, -*chū*
means "in" (e.g., 空気中 *kūki-chū* "in the air") or
"among" (e.g., 例外中 *reigai-chū* "among exceptions").
Although *jū* "entire, throughout" (q.v.) is etymologically
related and written with the same *kanji*, it is best thought
of as a separate item (Martin 1975: 881).

Accent: unaccented.

(1) 連敗中 *renpai-chū* "in a losing streak"

BASE: 連敗 *renpai* "straight losses."

連敗中の巨人は元気がない。

Renpai-chū no Kyojin wa genki ga nai.

In the midst of a losing streak, the Giants are in the doldrums.

(2) 漂流中 *hyōryū-chū* "while adrift."

BASE: 漂流 *hyōryū* "drifting."

難民は漂流中、雨水をためて飲んだ。

Nanmin wa hyōryū-chū, amamizu o tamete nonda.

While the refugees were adrift, they collected rainwater and
　drank it.

(3) 建築中 *kenchiku-chū* "under construction."

BASE: 建築 *kenchiku* "construction."

新宿の駅ビルは今建築中だ。

Shinjuku no eki-biru wa ima kenchiku-chū da.

The station building at Shinjuku is now under construction.

(4) 考慮中 *kōryo-chū* "under consideration."

BASE: 考慮 *kōryo* "consideration."

私は今でもその問題を考慮中だ。
Watashi wa ima de mo sono mondai o kōryo-chū da.
I still have that problem under consideration.

(5) 故障中 *koshō-chū* "out of order."

BASE: 故障 *koshō* "breakdown."

自動販売機に「故障中」という紙が貼ってある。
Jidō-hanbai-ki ni "koshō-chū" to iu kami ga hatte aru.
There is a paper stuck on the vending machine that says "out of order."

(6) 妊娠中 *ninshin-chū* "pregnant."

BASE: 妊娠 *ninshin* "pregnancy."

妊娠中の女性は酒を飲まない方がいい。
Ninshin-chū no josei wa sake o nomanai hō ga ii.
Pregnant women shouldn't drink alcoholic beverages.

(7) 来月中 *raigetsu-chū* "during next month."

BASE: 来月 *raigetsu* "next month."

部長は来月中に大阪へ出かける。
Buchō wa raigetsu-chū ni Ōsaka e dekakeru.
The department head is going to Osaka next month.

(8) 連載中 *rensai-chū* "during the appearance of a series."

BASE: 連載 *rensai* "appearing as a series."

その作家は小説の連載中に病気になった。
Sono sakka wa shōsetsu no rensai-chū ni byōki ni natta.
That writer became ill while his novel was being serialized.

(9) 点滴中 *tenteki-chū* "on an I.V."

BASE: 点滴 *tenteki* "intravenous drip."

患者はまだ点滴中だ。
Kanja wa mada tenteki-chū da.
The patient is still on an I.V.

(10) 雑談中 *zatsudan-chū* "during a chat."

BASE: 雑談 *zatsudan* "chat."

雑談中、彼は大声で笑った。

Zatsudan-chū, kare wa ōgoe de waratta.
In the midst of the chat, he laughed in a loud voice.

勤務 *kinmu* "duty, work."	仕事 *shigoto* "work."
勤務中 *kinmu-chū* "on duty."	仕事中 *shigoto-chū*
工事 *kōji*	"working, while working."
"construction work, repair."	会議 *kaigi* "conference."
工事中 *kōji-chū*	会議中 *kaigi-chū*
"under construction, repair."	"in conference."

Approximate English Equivalents:
charge, cost.

A word formed with *-dai* denotes money paid in exchange for what is specified by the base. The base typically specifies something which is bought (examples 1, 3, 5). In other cases, the base denotes something which is used temporarily, such as a mode of transportation or a place to live (example 2). There are also examples in which the base denotes an action (example 4), usually some kind of manual labor. In range of use, *-dai* overlaps with ‒費 *-hi* (q.v.), ‒料 *-ryō* (q.v.), ‒金 *-kin* (q.v.), and ‒賃 *-chin* (not included). For details, see Kimura (1986). The use of *-chin* seems to be restricted to bases denoting a vehicle or some kind of manual labor, and words with this element have an old-fashioned ring (Kimura 1986: 101).

Accent: unaccented.

(1) ガラス代 *garasu-dai* "glass cost."

BASE: ガラス *garasu* "glass."

窓ガラスを割った少年はあやまりながらガラス代を払った。
Mado-garasu o watta shōnen wa ayamarinagara garasu-dai o haratta.
The boy who broke the window apologized as he paid the cost of the glass.

(2) 部屋代 *heya-dai* "room rent."

BASE: 部屋 *heya* "room."

この辺のアパートなら、部屋代は月に10万円くらいだ。

Kono hen no apāto nara, heya-dai wa tsuki ni jū-man-en kurai da.

For an apartment around here, the rent is about ¥100,000 a month.

(3) 薬代 *kusuri-dai* "medicine costs."

BASE: 薬 *kusuri* "medicine."

薬代が高くてしょうがない。

Kusuri-dai ga takakute shō ga nai.

The cost of medicine is too much for words.

(4) 修理代 *shūri-dai* "repair charge."

BASE: 修理 *shūri* "repair."

彼女は車の修理代で困っていた。

Kanojo wa kuruma no shūri-dai de komatte ita.

She was in a fix about the repair charges for the car.

(5) 灯油代 *tōyu-dai* "kerosene cost."

BASE: 灯油 *tōyu* "kerosene."

今年は灯油代が値上がりした。

Kotoshi wa tōyu-dai ga ne-agari shita.

The price of kerosene went up this year.

昼食 *chūshoku* "lunch."	ホテル *hoteru* "hotel."
昼食代 *chūshoku-dai* "cost of lunch."	ホテル代 *hoteru-dai* "hotel charges."
電気 *denki* "electricity."	新聞 *shinbun* "newspaper."
電気代 *denki-dai* "electricity charges."	新聞代 *shinbun-dai* "cost of (subscription fee for) a newspaper."

DAN

Approximate English Equivalents: group, team.

A word formed with *-dan* denotes an organized group of people who participate in some activity together. The base may denote the kind of person in the group (examples 7, 9) or the activity (examples 1–6, 8, 10). The use of *-dan* is broader than, but overlaps with, the use of 隊 -tai (q.v.).

Accent: ⌐-dan.

(1) 弁護団 bengo-dan ''defense lawyer team.''

BASE: 弁護 bengo ''(legal) defense.''

弁護団はその判決に不満だった。

Bengo-dan wa sono hanketsu ni fuman datta.

The defense lawyers were dissatisfied with that decision.

(2) 暴力団 bōryoku-dan ''gang (of thugs).''

BASE: 暴力 bōryoku ''violence.''

最近、暴力団の争いが多くなってきた。

Saikin, bōryoku-dan no arasoi ga ōku natte kita.

Disputes between gangs have increased recently.

(3) 陳情団 chinjō-dan ''lobbying group.''

BASE: 陳情 chinjō ''lobbying.''

あの議員は陳情団に弱い。

Ano giin wa chinjō-dan ni yowai.

That Diet member is easily swayed by lobbying groups.

(4) 訪米団 hōbei-dan ''delegation to the U.S.''

BASE: 訪米 hōbei ''visiting the U.S.''

政府の訪米団は31日に出発する。

Seifu no hōbei-dan wa sanjūichi-nichi ni shuppatsu suru.

The government delegation to the United States will leave on the
  thirty-first.

(5) 調査団 chōsa-dan ''investigating commission.''

BASE: 調査 chōsa ''investigation.''

調査団は詳しくその事故を調べた。

Chōsa-dan wa kuwashiku sono jiko o shirabeta.

The investigating commission investigated the accident in detail.

(6) 応援団 ōen-dan ''cheering group.''

BASE: 応援 ōen ''cheering.''

応援団は試合中ずっと立っていた。

Ōen-dan wa shiai-chū zutto tatte ita.

The cheering section was standing all during the game.

(7) 選手団 senshu-dan ''athletic team.''

BASE: 選手 *senshu* "athlete."

キューバの選手団は1988年のオリンピックには参加しなかった。
Kyūba no senshu-dan wa senkyūhyaku-hachijūhachi-nen no Orinpikku ni wa sanka shinakatta.
Cuba's team did not participate in the 1988 Olympics.

(8) 視察団 *shisatsu-dan* "inspection team."

BASE: 視察 *shisatsu* "inspection."

昨日、視察団から報告書が届いた。
Sakujitsu, shisatsu-dan kara hōkoku-sho ga todoita.
Yesterday a report arrived from the inspection team.

(9) 少年団 *shōnen-dan* "boys' group."

BASE: 少年 *shōnen* "young boy."

ボーイ・スカウトのような少年団はいろいろある。
Bōi-sukauto no yō na shōnen-dan wa iroiro aru.
There are all sorts of boys' groups like the Boy Scouts.

(10) 観光団 *kankō-dan* "tourist group."

BASE: 観光 *kankō* "tourism."

ハワイは日本人の観光団であふれている。
Hawai wa Nihon-jin no kankō-dan de afurete iru.
Hawaii is overflowing with Japanese tourist groups.

合唱 *gasshō* "singing together."	使節 *shisetsu* "envoy, delegate."
合唱団 *gasshō-dan* "chorus, choir."	使節団 *shisetsu-dan* "delegation."
記者 *kisha* "reporter."	医師 *ishi* "doctor."
記者団 *kisha-dan* "reporter group, press corps."	医師団 *ishi-dan* "team of doctors."

度
DO

Approximate English Equivalents:
degree, -ness.

A word formed with *-do* denotes the degree to which the property specified by the base is present. In range, while *-do* overlaps with 一性 *-sei* (q.v.), *-do* is more specific. Even when it denotes a property that has gradations, a word with -*sei* can be used to mean that property in the abstract or the simple presence of that property rather than the degree to which it is present. Compare 安定性 *antei-sei* (stability) with 安定度 *antei-do* (degree of stability).

Accent: ⌐-*do*.

(1) 完成度 *kansei-do* "degree of completeness or perfection."
BASE: 完成 *kansei* "completion, perfection."
我々は完成度の高い車を生産したい。
Wareware wa kansei-do no takai kuruma o seisan shitai.
We want to produce cars that are nearly perfect.

(2) 重要度 *jūyō-do* "degree of importance."
BASE: 重要 *jūyō (na)* "important."
コンピューターの重要度はますます高くなっている。
Konpyūtā no jūyō-do wa masumasu takaku natte iru.
The importance of the computer has grown steadily.

(3) 燃焼度 *nenshō-do* "degree of combustibility."
BASE: 燃焼 *nenshō* "combustion."
この車には燃焼度の高いアルコールが使われている。
Kono kuruma ni wa nenshō-do no takai arukōru ga tsukawarete iru.
This car uses highly combustible alcohol.

(4) 酸性度 *sansei-do* "degree of acidity."
BASE: 酸性 *sansei* "acidity."
酸性度の強い雨が問題になっている。
Sansei-do no tsuyoi ame ga mondai ni natte iru.
Rain with a high degree of acidity has become a problem.

(5) 透明度 *tōmei-do* "degree of transparency."
BASE: 透明 *tōmei (na)* "transparent."
ダイヤモンドの品質は透明度で決まる。
Daiyamondo no hinshitsu wa tōmei-do de kimaru.
A diamond's quality is determined by its transparency.

アルコール　*arukōru* "alcohol."　　信頼　*shinrai* "trust, reliance."
アルコール度　*arukōru-do*　　　　信頼度　*shinrai-do*
　　"degree (percent) of alcohol."　　　　"degree of trust."

加速 *kasoku* "acceleration."	適応 *tekiō* "adaptation."
加速度 *kasoku-do*	適応度 *tekiō-do*
"rate of acceleration."	"degree of adaptation."

FŪ

Approximate English Equivalents: -style, -like, -looking.

A word formed with *-fū* means the appearance or air of what is denoted by the base. It can be followed by *no* and used as a noun modifier (examples 1, 4, 5), followed by *ni* and used adverbially (example 2), or followed by a form of *da* and used as a predicate (example 3). (It is not uncommon, however, to see a word with *-fū* used as an adjectival noun, with *na*.) The base typically denotes a person or group (example 1), a place (examples 4, 5), or an era (examples 2, 3). In range of use, *-fū* overlaps with 一式 *-shiki* (q.v.) and 一的 *-teki* (q.v.), but a resemblance specified by a word with *-shiki* is genuine rather than apparent (Arakawa 1986: 89), and a resemblance specified by a word with *-teki* can be either genuine or apparent. Semantically closer to *-fū* are 一流 *-ryū* (q.v.), 一調 *-chō* (q.v.), and 一然 *-zen* (not included). There are also examples in which *-fū* has its literal meaning of "wind": 貿易風 *bōeki-fū* (trade wind), 季節風 *kisetsu-fū* (seasonal wind).

Accent: unaccented.

(1) 学生風 *gakusei-fū (no)* "with the look of a student."

BASE: 学生 *gakusei* "student."

犯人は学生風の男だった。
Hannin wa gakusei-fū no otoko datta.
The criminal was a man with the look of a student about him.

(2) 現代風 *gendai-fū (no)* "modern style."

BASE: 現代 *gendai* "modern times, the present day, today."

若い人たちは現代風に手紙を横書きにする。
Wakai hitotachi wa gendai-fū ni tegami o yokogaki ni suru.
Young people write letters in a modern way, from left to right.

(3) ルネッサンス風 *Runessansu-fū (no)* "Renaissance-style."

BASE: ルネッサンス *Runessansu* "Renaissance."

あの建物はルネッサンス風だ。
Ano tatemono wa Runessansu-fū da.
That building is in the Renaissance style.

(4) 西洋風 *Seiyō-fū (no)* "Western-style."

BASE: 西洋 *Seiyō* "the Occident."

日本には西洋風のレストランがあふれている。
Nihon ni wa Seiyō-fū no resutoran ga afurete iru.
Japan is overflowing with Western-style restaurants.

(5) 都会風 *tokai-fū (no)* "city-like, urban."

BASE: 都会 *tokai* "city."

都会風の店が新しくできた。
Tokai-fū no mise ga atarashiku dekita.
A store with an urban atmosphere has newly opened.

中国 *Chūgoku* "China."	労働者 *rōdō-sha* "worker."	
中国風 *Chūgoku-fū (no)* "Chinese-style."	労働者風 *rōdō-sha-fū (no)* "worker-like."	
田舎 *inaka* "the country."	紳士 *shinshi* "gentleman."	
田舎風 *inaka-fū (no)* "country-style."	紳士風 *shinshi-fū (no)* "gentleman-like."	

派
HA

Approximate English Equivalents:
group, faction, school, sect.

A word formed with *-ha* denotes a group of people who identify with or favor what is denoted by the base. The word also implies the existence of one or more opposing or contrasting groups, and it is not unusual for the other group(s) to be mentioned explicitly (example 3). The *-ha* pattern is typically used to name artistic or academic schools (example 2), political factions or camps (examples 1, 7, 9), and religious sects or denominations (example 4). It is also used to coin names for types of people defined by some shared interest, preference, characteristic, etc. (examples 3, 5, 6, 8, 10), and this use overlaps with the range of use of −層 *-sō* (q.v.), −族 *-zoku* (not included), and −閥 *-batsu* (not included).

Accent: unaccented.

(1) 保守派 *hoshu-ha* "conservative faction."

BASE: 保守 *hoshu* "conservatism."

彼は保守派のリーダーとして有名だ。
Kare wa hoshu-ha no rīdā to shite yūmei da.
He is famous as the leader of the conservative faction.

(2) 印象派 *inshō-ha* "Impressionist school."

BASE: 印象 *inshō* "impression."

「印象派」と言えばモネを思い出す。
"Inshō-ha" to ieba Mone o omoidasu.
If you mention the Impressionists, I can't help thinking of Monet.

(3) レコード派 *rekōdo-ha* "those who prefer records."

BASE: レコード *rekōdo* "phonographic record."

ときどきレコード派はCD派をバカにする。
Tokidoki rekōdo-ha wa shīdī-ha o baka ni suru.
Record buffs sometimes make fun of the CD crowd.

(4) 改革派 *kaikaku-ha* "reform sect."

BASE: 改革 *kaikaku* "reform."

最近、ユダヤ教の改革派が増えている。
Saikin, Yudaya-kyō no Kaikaku-ha ga fuete iru.
Recently the Reform sect of Judaism has grown.

(5) 国際派 *kokusai-ha* "cosmopolitan people."

BASE: 国際 *kokusai* "international intercourse."

外国語ができても国際派とは限らない。
Gaikoku-go ga dekite mo kokusai-ha to wa kagiranai.
Just being able to speak a foreign language doesn't necessarily make you a cosmopolitan.

(6) 拒否派 *kyohi-ha* "those who reject."

BASE: 拒否 *kyohi* "rejection."

彼の息子も大学拒否派だった。

Kare no musuko mo daigaku-kyohi-ha datta.
His son was also one of those who rejected college.

(7) ニューディール派 *Nyūdīru-ha* "New Dealers."

BASE: ニューディール *Nyūdīru* "the New Deal."

ＧＨＱにはニューディール派が多かった。
Jī-etchi-kyū ni wa Nyūdīru-ha ga ōkatta.
In GHQ there were many New Dealers.

(8) 戦後派 *sengo-ha* "those born after World War II."

BASE: 戦後 *sengo* "the postwar."

戦後派がもっと増えれば日本は変わるだろう。
Sengo-ha ga motto fuereba Nihon wa kawaru darō.
As the number of people born after the war increases, Japan will
surely change.

(9) 田中派 *Tanaka-ha* "the Tanaka faction."

BASE: 田中 *Tanaka* (a common surname).

田中派は今でも自民党で一番強いかもしれない。
*Tanaka-ha wa ima de mo Jimin-tō de ichiban tsuyoi ka mo
shirenai.*
Even now, the Tanaka faction may be the strongest in the
Liberal-Democratic Party.

(10) 体制派 *taisei-ha* "members of the Establishment."

BASE: 体制 *taisei* "system, the Establishment."

彼は若いとき体制派が嫌いだった。
Kare wa wakai toki taisei-ha ga kirai datta.
In his youth he disliked the Establishment.

過激　*kageki (na)* "extreme."	穏健　*onken (na)* "moderate."
過激派　*kageki-ha* "extremists."	穏健派　*onken-ha* "moderates."
進歩　*shinpo* "progress."	鷹　*taka* "hawk."
進歩派　*shinpo-ha* "progressives."	鷹派　*taka-ha* "hawks, hard-liners."

費
HI

Approximate English Equivalents:
cost, expense, expenditure.

A word formed with *-hi* denotes an expenditure for what is specified by the base. The base typically denotes an activity (examples 1, 2, 5), but there are also examples in which the base denotes an organization (example 3) or some broad category of supplies or equipment (example 4). In range of use, *-hi* overlaps with 金 *-kin* (q.v.) and 代 *-dai* (q.v.). For details, see Kimura (1986). Unlike *-hi*, *-dai* tends to be added to bases that denote concrete objects rather than generic categories. In addition, *-hi* almost always occurs with bases of Chinese origin, whereas *-dai* occurs freely with bases that are native Japanese words or recent loanwords. A few words with *-hi* are quite different from the examples treated here; the base describes the manner in which the expense is incurred or the expenditure is made (Kimura 1986: 103): 臨時費 *rinji-hi* (incidental expense).

Accent: ⌐*-hi*.

(1) 防衛費 *bōei-hi* ''defense expenditures.''

BASE: 防衛 *bōei* ''defense.''

この10年間で防衛費はだいぶ増えた。

Kono jū-nenkan de bōei-hi wa daibu fueta.

Defense expenditures have increased considerably in the last ten years.

(2) 維持費 *iji-hi* ''maintenance expenses.''

BASE: 維持 *iji* ''maintenance.''

博物館の維持費は県が出している。

Hakubutsu-kan no iji-hi wa ken ga dashite iru.

Maintenance expenses for the museum are paid by the prefecture.

(3) 組合費 *kumiai-hi* ''union dues.''

BASE: 組合 *kumiai* ''union.''

組合費は給料から差し引かれる。

Kumiai-hi wa kyūryō kara sashihikareru.

Union dues are deducted from salary.

(4) 燃料費 *nenryō-hi* "fuel costs."

BASE: 燃料 *nenryō* "fuel."

燃料費が高くなったので航空会社が次々につぶれた。

Nenryō-hi ga takaku natta no de kōkū-gaisha ga tsugitsugi ni tsubureta.

With the rise in fuel costs, airlines folded one after another.

(5) 生活費 *seikatsu-hi* "living expenses."

BASE: 生活 *seikatsu* "living."

生活費の足りない学生が多い。

Seikatsu-hi no tarinai gakusei ga ōi.

Many students don't have enough money for living expenses.

医療	*iryō* "medical treatment."	交通	*kōtsū* "transportation."
医療費	*iryō-hi* "medical expenses."	交通費	*kōtsū-hi* "transportation expenses."
建築	*kenchiku* "construction (of buildings)."	生産	*seisan* "production."
建築費	*kenchiku-hi* "construction costs."	生産費	*seisan-hi* "production costs."

Approximate English Equivalents: article, item, object.

A word formed with *-hin* denotes an object of a type specified by the base. The range of use of *-hin* overlaps with that of 一物 *-butsu* (q.v.), but a word with *-hin* always denotes a countable object that has been made or processed by someone. The object is often some sort of merchandise.

Accent: unaccented.

(1) 美術品 *bijutsu-hin* "art object."

BASE: 美術 *bijutsu* "art."

この画廊には多くの美術品が並べてある。

Kono garō ni wa ōku no bijutsu-hin ga narabete aru.

Many art objects are set out at this gallery.

(2) 不良品 *furyō-hin* "defective item."

BASE: 不良 *furyō (na)* "badness."

この工場は不良品が少ないことで有名だ。
Kono kōjō wa furyō-hin ga sukunai koto de yūmei da.
This factory is famous for producing very few defective items.

(3) メーカー品 *mēkā-hin* "brand-name item."

BASE: メーカー *mēkā* "manufacturer."

このデパートにはメーカー品がそろっている。
Kono depāto ni wa mēkā-hin ga sorotte iru.
They have all the brand-name items at this department store.

(4) 輸入品 *yunyū-hin* "imported item."

BASE: 輸入 *yunyū* "importing."

輸入品は毎年増えている。
Yunyū-hin wa mainen fuete iru.
Imported items are increasing every year.

(5) 贅沢品 *zeitaku-hin* "luxury item."

BASE: 贅沢 *zeitaku / ~ (na)* "luxury / extravagant."

新しい政府は贅沢品の税金を重くした。
Atarashii seifu wa zeitaku-hin no zeikin o omoku shita.
The new government placed a heavier tax on luxury items.

代用 *daiyō* "substitution."	身の回り *mi-no-mawari* "one's person."	
代用品 *daiyō-hin* "substitute item."	身の回り品 *mi-no-mawari-hin* "personal belongings."	
規格 *kikaku* "a standard."		
規格品 *kikaku-hin* "a standardized article."	装飾 *sōshoku* "ornamentation."	
	装飾品 *sōshoku-hin* "ornament."	

法
HŌ

Approximate English Equivalents:
method, way.

A word formed with *-hō* denotes a method or way of doing what is denoted by the base. The base must therefore denote something that can be construed as an activity. However, there are also examples of a different pattern,

58

one in which the word formed with *-hō* denotes a label for some particular method: 複利法 *fukuri-hō* (the method of compound interest) and メートル法 *mētoru-hō* (the metric system). Although *-hō* "law" is etymologically related and is written with the same *kanji*, it is best thought of as a separate item.

Accent: unaccented.

(1) 治療法 *chiryō-hō* "treatment method."

BASE: 治療 *chiryō* "medical treatment."

この病院の治療法は遅れているらしい。

Kono byōin no chiryō-hō wa okurete iru rashii.

This hospital's methods of treatment seem to be behind the times.

(2) 発想法 *hassō-hō* "way of conceiving things."

BASE: 発想 *hassō* "(mental) conception."

物理学者の発想法は普通の人と違う。

Butsuri-gakusha no hassō-hō wa futsū no hito to chigau.

The way physicists conceive of things is different from the way ordinary people do.

(3) 避妊法 *hinin-hō* "method of contraception."

BASE: 避妊 *hinin* "contraception."

避妊法は戦後普及した。

Hinin-hō wa sengo fukyū shita.

Methods of contraception spread after the war.

(4) 表現法 *hyōgen-hō* "method of expression."

BASE: 表現 *hyōgen* "expression."

日本語の表現法には難しいところがある。

Nihon-go no hyōgen-hō ni wa muzukashii tokoro ga aru.

The Japanese language has some difficult methods of expression.

(5) 栽培法 *saibai-hō* "method of cultivation."

BASE: 栽培 *saibai* "cultivation."

トマトの新しい栽培法が見つかった。

Tomato no atarashii saibai-hō ga mitsukatta.

A new method of cultivating tomatoes has been found.

(6) 解決法 *kaiketsu-hō* ''method of resolution.''

BASE: 解決 *kaiketsu* ''resolution.''

残念ながら、これは一時的な解決法に過ぎない。
Zannen-nagara, kore wa ichiji-teki na kaiketsu-hō ni suginai.
Unfortunately, this is just a temporary solution.

(7) 解消法 *kaishō-hō* ''elimination method.''

BASE: 解消 *kaishō* ''elimination, cancellation.''

スポーツをすることは、ひとつのストレス解消法だ。
Supōtsu o suru koto wa, hitotsu no sutoresu-kaishō-hō da.
Playing sports is one method of eliminating stress.

(8) 使用法 *shiyō-hō* ''method of use.''

BASE: 使用 *shiyō* ''use.''

薬を使うときは、使用法をよく確かめるべきだ。
Kusuri o tsukau toki wa, shiyō-hō o yoku tashikameru beki da.
When taking medicine, check the instructions carefully.

(9) 説明法 *setsumei-hō* ''way of explaining.''

BASE: 説明 *setsumei* ''explanation.''

スライドを使った説明法は優れている。
Suraido o tsukatta setsumei-hō wa sugurete iru.
The use of slides is an excellent method of explanation.

(10) 予防法 *yobō-hō* ''prevention method.''

BASE: 予防 *yobō* ''prevention.''

かぜの予防法として決定的なものはまだない。
Kaze no yobō-hō toshite kettei-teki na mono wa mada nai.
There is still no foolproof method of preventing colds.

分類	*bunrui* ''classification.''	思考	*shikō* ''thinking.''
分類法	*bunrui-hō* ''classification system.''	思考法	*shikō-hō* ''way of thinking.''
営業	*eigyō* ''business.''	測定	*sokutei* ''measurement.''
営業法	*eigyō-hō* ''way of doing business.''	測定法	*sokutei-hō* ''measuring method.''

員
IN

Approximate English Equivalents: member, -er.

A word formed with -*in* is a noun denoting a person who is a member of some organized group. In some cases, the base denotes the group itself (examples 2, 6), and bases containing 一部 -*bu* (q.v.), 一団 -*dan* (q.v.), or 一隊 -*tai* (q.v.) are common. In other cases, the base denotes the activity in which the group members are involved. The group is often a business or government organization, and in such examples the word with -*in* typically denotes an employee. In range of use, -*in* overlaps with 一者 -*sha* (q.v.) and with 一工 -*kō* (q.v.), although -*sha* and -*kō* are not added to bases denoting groups. In addition, -*sha* lacks the explicit meaning of group affiliation (e.g., 指導者 *shidō-sha* "leader" vs. 指導員 *shidō-in* "supervisor"), and -*kō* implies factory work (e.g., 整備工 *seibi-kō* / 整備員 *seibi-in* "maintenance worker.").

Accent: ⁻-*in*.

(1) 調査員 *chōsa-in* "survey taker."
BASE: 調査 *chōsa* "survey."
投票所の外に調査員が立っていた。
Tōhyō-jo no soto ni chōsa-in ga tatte ita.
Survey takers were standing outside the polling places.

(2) 劇団員 *gekidan-in* "drama troupe member."
BASE: 劇団 *gekidan* "drama troupe."
劇団員の1人が急に病気になった。
Gekidan-in no hitori ga kyū ni byōki ni natta.
One member of the drama troupe suddenly got sick.

(3) 販売員 *hanbai-in* "salesperson."
BASE: 販売 *hanbai* "selling."
化粧品の販売員は深くおじぎをした。
Keshō-hin no hanbai-in wa fukaku ojigi o shita.
The cosmetics salesperson bowed deeply.

(4) 従業員 *jūgyō-in* "employee."

BASE: 従業 *jūgyō* "working."

我が社の従業員はみんな幸せだ。

Wagasha no jūgyō-in wa minna shiawase da.

All of the employees at our company are happy.

(5) 警備員 *keibi-in* "guard."

BASE: 警備 *keibi* "guarding."

この銀行の警備員には元警察官が多い。

Kono ginkō no keibi-in ni wa moto-keisatsu-kan ga ōi.

Among the guards at this bank, there are many former police officers.

(6) 機動隊員 *kidō-tai-in* "riot policeman."

BASE: 機動隊 *kidō-tai* "riot squad."

そのデモでは学生10人と機動隊員3人が怪我をした。

Sono demo de wa gakusei jū-nin to kidō-tai-in san-nin ga kega o shita.

At that demonstration, ten students and three riot policemen were hurt.

(7) 公務員 *kōmu-in* "public employee."

BASE: 公務 *kōmu* "public service."

国立大学の教授は公務員だ。

Kokuritsu-daigaku no kyōju wa kōmu-in da.

Professors at national universities are public employees.

(8) 乗組員 *norikumi-in* "crew member."

BASE: 乗り組み *norikumi* "serving as crew."

この船の乗組員はほとんどフィリピン人だ。

Kono fune no norikumi-in wa hotondo Firipin-jin da.

This ship's crew is almost entirely Filipino.

(9) 審査員 *shinsa-in* "judge, examiner, inspector."

BASE: 審査 *shinsa* "judging."

文学賞では，ときどき審査員の意見が大きく分かれることがある。

Bungaku-shō de wa, tokidoki shinsa-in no iken ga ōkiku wakareru koto ga aru.

The judges for literary awards are sometimes greatly divided in opinion.

(10) 相談員 *sōdan-in* "counselor."

BASE: 相談 *sōdan* "consultation."

彼女は老人問題の相談員をしている。
Kanojo wa rōjin-mondai no sōdan-in o shite iru.
She is acting as a counselor on problems concerning the aged.

銀行 *ginkō* "bank."   会社 *kaisha* "company."
銀行員 *ginkō-in*   会社員 *kaisha-in*
   "bank employee."   "company employee."

組合 *kumiai* "union.."   研究 *kenkyū* "research."
組合員 *kumiai-in*   研究員 *kenkyū-in* "researcher."
   "union member."

人 JIN

Approximate English Equivalents:
person, inhabitant.

A word formed with *-jin* denotes a person who belongs to a subgroup of the human race specified by the base. This element is best known for its regular occurrence with bases denoting a country (as in カナダ人 *Kanada-jin* "a Canadian") or an ethnic group (as in アイヌ人 *Ainu-jin* "Ainu person"), but it has a wider range of use. Nonetheless, it appears that the base can always be interpreted as specifying a subgroup of humanity. In some cases the base specifies a literal place or era (examples 2, 4). In other cases, the base specifies a figurative realm, either by denoting the realm itself (examples 8, 10) or some feature of the realm (examples 1, 5, 6, 7, 9). In still other cases, the base specifies a shared attribute that defines membership in the subgroup (example 3). Although *-nin* "person, -er" (q.v.) is etymologically related and written with the same *kanji*, it is best thought of as a separate item.

Accent: ⌐*-jin*.

(1) 知識人 *chishiki-jin* "intellectual."

BASE: 知識 *chishiki* "knowledge."

知識人の知識は本から得ることが多い。

Chishiki-jin no chishiki wa hon kara eru koto ga ōi.
The knowledge of intellectuals is often acquired from books.

(2) 現地人 *genchi-jin* "local person."

BASE: 現地 *genchi* "locale."

現地人との労使関係はむずかしかった。
Genchi-jin to no rōshi-kankei wa muzukashikatta.
Labor-management relations with the local people were difficult.

(3) 一般人 *ippan-jin* "ordinary person."

BASE: 一般 *ippan (no)* "general."

そのデモには学生ばかりでなく一般人も参加した。
*Sono demo ni wa gakusei bakari de naku ippan-jin mo sanka
    shita.*
Not only students, but ordinary people also took part in that
    demonstration.

(4) 現代人 *gendai-jin* "modern person."

BASE: 現代 *gendai* "modern times."

現代人はいつもストレスと闘っている。
Gendai-jin wa itsu mo sutoresu to tatakatte iru.
Modern people are always struggling with stress.

(5) 経済人 *keizai-jin* "business leader."

BASE: 経済 *keizai* "economy."

政府は学者や経済人に意見を求めた。
Seifu wa gakusha ya keizai-jin ni iken o motometa.
The government sought the opinion of scholars and business
    leaders.

(6) 民間人 *minkan-jin* "civilian."

BASE: 民間 *minkan (no)* "civil, private."

首都では民間人を含めて2000人が殺された。
Shuto de wa minkan-jin o fukumete nisen-nin ga korosareta.
In the capital, 2,000 people were killed, including civilians.

(7) 国際人 *kokusai-jin* "cosmopolitan."

BASE: 国際 *kokusai* "international intercourse."

これからは子供たちを本当の国際人にするべきだ。
*Kore kara wa kodomo-tachi o hontō no kokusai-jin ni suru beki
    da.*

From now on we must make our children true cosmopolitans.

(8) 社会人 *shakai-jin* "full member of society."

BASE: 社会 *shakai* "society."

日本では二十歳になると社会人だといわれる。

Nihon de wa hatachi ni naru to shakai-jin da to iwareru.

In Japan, when you turn twenty, you are said to be a full-fledged member of society.

(9) 新聞人 *shinbun-jin* "newspaper person."

BASE: 新聞 *shinbun* "newspaper."

上田氏は反骨の新聞人だった。

Ueda-shi wa hankotsu no shinbun-jin datta.

Mr. Ueda was an uncompromising newspaperman.

(10) 財界人 *zaikai-jin* "financier."

BASE: 財界 *zaikai* "the financial world."

新しい政策は財界人に非難された。

Atarashii seisaku wa zaikai-jin ni hinan sareta.

The new government policy was condemned by financiers.

文化 *bunka* "culture."	都会 *tokai* "city."
文化人 *bunka-jin* "cultured person."	都会人 *tokai-jin* "city dweller."
外国 *gaikoku* "foreign country."	有名 *yūmei (na)* "famous."
外国人 *gaikoku-jin* "foreigner."	有名人 *yūmei-jin* "celebrity."

所
JO / SHO

Approximate English Equivalents:
place, facility.

A word formed with *-jo* or *-sho* denotes a place where people carry out an activity specified by the base. The range of use of *-jo / -sho* overlaps with that of 一場 *-jō* (q.v.), and some bases can occur with either, but there seems to be a preference for *-jo / -sho* when the activity is relatively sedentary (Nakagawa 1986: 107–108) or involves a relatively small number of people. It appears that *-jo* and *-sho* are entirely synonymous. Which of the two will occur with a given base is not predictable, although *-jo* is more common (Nakagawa 1986: 106). In many cases, both are possible (examples 1, 2, 3).

Accent: unaccented.

(1) 案内所 *annai-jo / -sho* "information office."
BASE: 案内 *annai* "information."
彼らは案内所で道をたずねた。
Karera wa annai-jo de michi o tazuneta.
They asked directions at the information office.

(2) 保健所 *hoken-jo / -sho* "health center."
BASE: 保健 *hoken* "health preservation."
彼女は気分が悪くなって近くの保健所へ行った。
Kanojo wa kibun ga waruku natte chikaku no hoken-jo e itta.
She didn't feel well, and went to a nearby health center.

(3) 研究所 *kenkyū-jo / -sho* "research institute."
BASE: 研究 *kenkyū* "research."
コンピューター研究所は1969年にできた。
Konpyūtā-kenkyū-jo wa senkyūhyaku-rokujūkyū-nen ni dekita.
The computer research institute came into being in 1969.

(4) 裁判所 *saiban-sho* "court."
BASE: 裁判 *saiban* "trial."
被告人は裁判所に出かけた。

Hikoku-nin wa saiban-sho ni dekaketa.
The defendant left for the court.

(5) 投票所 *tōhyō-jo* "polling place."

BASE: 投票 *tōhyō* "voting."

選挙のとき、小学校は全部投票所になる。
Senkyo no toki, shōgakkō wa zenbu tōhyō-jo ni naru.
When there is an election, elementary schools all become polling
  places.

発電 *hatsuden*
  "electricity generation."
発電所 *hatsuden-jo / -sho*
  "power station."

事務 *jimu* "office work."
事務所 *jimu-sho* "office."

休憩 *kyūkei* "a rest, a break."
休憩所 *kyūkei-jo* "rest station."

撮影 *satsuei* "filming."
撮影所 *satsuei-jo*
  "movie studio."

Approximate English Equivalents:
place, facility.

A word formed with -*jō* denotes a place where people participate in an activity specified by the base. In range of use,
-*jō* overlaps with 所 -*jo / -sho* (q.v.), and some bases can
take either with no appreciable difference in meaning: 停留
場 *teiryū-jō* / 停留所 *teiryū-jo* (station, stop). Nonetheless, there seems to be a preference for -*jō* when the
activity denoted by the base is vigorous (Nakagawa 1986:
107–108) or involves a large number of people (Bunka-
chō 1975: 463).

Accent: unaccented.

(1) 駐車場 *chūsha-jō* "parking lot, parking garage."

BASE: 駐車 *chūsha* "parking."

一流ホテルには必ず駐車場がある。
Ichiryū-hoteru ni wa kanarazu chūsha-jō ga aru.
In a first-class hotel, there is invariably a parking garage.

(2) ゴルフ場 *gorufu-jō* "golf course."

BASE: ゴルフ *gorufu* "golf."

ゴルフ場は週末が一番混んでいる。
Gorufu-jō wa shūmatsu ga ichiban konde iru.
Golf courses are most crowded on weekends.

(3) 飛行場 *hikō-jō* "airport."

BASE: 飛行 *hikō* "aviation."

東京駅から飛行場までは1時間ぐらいかかる。
Tōkyō-eki kara hikō-jō made wa ichijikan-gurai kakaru.
It takes about an hour from Tokyo Station to the airport.

(4) 競技場 *kyōgi-jō* "stadium, athletic field."

BASE: 競技 *kyōgi* "competition."

たいていの大学は競技場を持っている。
Taitei no daigaku wa kyōgi-jō o motte iru.
Most universities have an athletic field.

(5) 養魚場 *yōgyo-jō* "fish farm."

BASE: 養魚 *yōgyo* "fish farming."

彼女はこの5年間養魚場で働いている。
Kanojo wa kono go-nenkan yōgyo-jō de hataraite iru.
She has been working at a fish farm for the last five years.

運動 *undō* "movement, exercise."	スケート *sukēto* "skating."
運動場 *undō-jō* "playground, athletic field, gym."	スケート場 *sukēto-jō* "skating rink."
試験 *shiken* "exam."	会議 *kaigi* "conference."
試験場 *shiken-jō* "exam hall."	会議場 *kaigi-jō* "conference hall."

JŌ

Approximate English Equivalents:
pertaining to, -al(ly), -wise.

A word formed with *-jō* can function as an adverb meaning "from the standpoint of," "as a matter of," "for the sake of" what is denoted by the base (examples 2, 4, 5, 6, 9). In this use, *-jō* can be paraphrased as の上で *no ue de*.

When followed by *no*, a word with *-jō* functions as a noun modifier meaning "pertaining to" what is denoted by the base (examples 1, 3, 7, 8, 10), and *-jō* can be paraphrased as の上 *no ue*. There are also words of a different type in which *-jō* has its literal meaning of "on" or "above": 地球上 *chikyū-jō* "on earth."

Accent: unaccented.

(1) 文法上 *bunpō-jō (no)* "grammatical."

BASE: 文法 *bunpō* "grammar."

彼の文章には文法上の誤りはない。
Kare no bunshō ni wa bunpō-jō no ayamari wa nai.
There are no grammatical errors in his writing.

(2) 外見上 *gaiken-jō (no)* "in terms of appearance."

BASE: 外見 *gaiken* "outward appearance."

形も色も同じだったので、外見上違いはなかった。
Katachi mo iro mo onaji datta no de, gaiken-jō chigai wa nakatta.
The shape and color were the same, so there was no difference as regards outward appearance.

(3) 学問上 *gakumon-jō (no)* "academic."

BASE: 学問 *gakumon* "learning, scholarship."

その2人は学問上のライバルだ。
Sono futari wa gakumon-jō no raibaru da.
Those two are academic rivals.

(4) 法律上 *hōritsu-jō (no)* "legal."

BASE: 法律 *hōritsu* "law."

彼のやったことは法律上問題はなかった。
Kare no yatta koto wa hōritsu-jō mondai wa nakatta.
Legally, there was nothing wrong in what he did.

(5) 競争上 *kyōsō-jō (no)* "for the sake of competition."

BASE: 競争 *kyōsō* "competition."

日本のメーカーとの競争上、GMも小型車を生産するようになった。
Nihon no mēkā to no kyōsō-jō, Jī-emu mo kogata-sha o seisan suru yō ni natta.

To compete with Japanese makers, GM began producing compacts too.

(6) 成り行き上 *nariyuki-jō (no)* "from the standpoint of the developments."

BASE: 成り行き *nariyuki* "the developments."

成り行き上、彼は会社をやめることになった。
Nariyuki-jō, kare wa kaisha o yameru koto ni natta.
In the course of events, he ended up quitting the company.

(7) 制度上 *seido-jō (no)* "institutional."

BASE: 制度 *seido* "system, institution."

制度上の差別がなくなっても、人間の心はなかなか変わらない。
Seido-jō no sabetsu ga nakunatte mo, ningen no kokoro wa nakanaka kawaranai.
Even if institutional discrimination disappears, people's hearts do not easily change.

(8) 戦術上 *senjutsu-jō (no)* "strategic."

BASE: 戦術 *senjutsu* "strategy."

あの攻撃は戦術上のミスだった。
Ano kōgeki wa senjutsu-jō no misu datta.
The attack was a strategic mistake.

(9) 商売上 *shōbai-jō (no)* "as regards business."

BASE: 商売 *shōbai* "business."

商売上はうまくいっているらしい。
Shōbai-jō wa umaku itte iru rashii.
As far as business is concerned, things seem to be going well.

(10) 財産上 *zaisan-jō (no)* "pertaining to assets."

BASE: 財産 *zaisan* "assets."

その会社は財産上の問題をたくさん抱えている。
Sono kaisha wa zaisan-jō no mondai o takusan kakaete iru.
That company has many problems concerning assets.

一身 *isshin* "oneself."	教育 *kyōiku* "education."
一身上 *isshin-jō (no)* "personal."	教育上 *kyōiku-jō (no)* "pertaining to education."
便宜 *bengi* "convenience."	意味 *imi* "meaning."
便宜上 *bengi-jō (no)* "for convenience."	意味上 *imi-jō (no)* "semantic."

中
JŪ

Approximate English Equivalents:
entire, throughout.

When the base denotes a period of time or an activity (examples 2, 4), a word formed with -*jū* means "throughout" the time period involved. Such a word can function as an adverb (example 2). When followed by *ni* (example 4), it means "at some point within" the time period involved (Martin 1975: 131). When the base denotes a place (examples 1, 3, 5), a word formed with -*jū* can function as an adverb meaning "all over" that place (example 3) or as a noun meaning "the entire extent" of that place (examples 1, 5). Although -*chū* "during, in the midst of" (q.v.) is etymologically related and written with the same *kanji*, it is best thought of as a separate item (Martin 1975: 881).

Accent: unaccented.

(1) 部屋中 *heya-jū* "all over the room."
BASE: 部屋 *heya* "room."
弁護士は部屋中を歩き回っていた。
Bengo-shi wa heya-jū o arukimawatte ita.
The lawyer was walking all around the room.

(2) 一晩中 *hitoban-jū* "all night."
BASE: 一晩 *hitoban* "one night."
彼は一晩中仕事をしていた。
Kare wa hitoban-jū shigoto o shite ita.
He was working all night.

(3) 顔中 *kao-jū* "entire face."
BASE: 顔 *kao* "face."
彼女は顔中涙で濡らしていた。
Kanojo wa kao-jū namida de nurashite ita.
Her entire face was wet with tears.

(4) 今週中 *konshū-jū* "throughout this week."
BASE: 今週 *konshū* "this week."
今週中にレポートを出すつもりだ。

Konshū-jū ni repōto o dasu tsumori da.
I plan to turn in the report sometime this week.

(5) 世界中 *sekai-jū* "the entire world."

BASE: 世界 *sekai* "world."

コカインはもうとっくに世界中に広がっている。
Kokain wa mō tokku ni sekai-jū ni hirogatte iru.
Cocaine has long since spread throughout the world.

学校 *gakkō* "school."	今日 *kyō* "today."
学校中 *gakkō-jū* "throughout the school."	今日中 *kyō-jū* "throughout today."
親戚 *shinseki* "a relation, a relative."	夏休み *natsuyasumi* "summer vacation."
親戚中 *shinseki-jū* "all the relations."	夏休み中 *natsuyasumi-jū* "throughout summer vaca- tion."

下
KA

Approximate English Equivalent:
under.

A word formed with *-ka* denotes a state of affairs in which
what is denoted by the base is in effect. Words with *-ka* can
be used adverbially by adding *de* (examples 1, 5). The
word *senji-ka* (example 4) is exceptional in this respect
since *de* is optional. There are also words of a different
type in which *-ka* is closer to its literal meaning of "below,
under": 意識下 *ishiki-ka (no)* (subconscious), 氷点下
hyōten-ka (no) (below freezing).

Accent: ⌐*-ka*.

(1) 影響下 *eikyō-ka* "under influence."

BASE: 影響 *eikyō* "influence."

彼はスターリンの影響下で政治を学んだ。
Kare wa Sutārin no eikyō-ka de seiji o mananda.
He learned about politics under Stalinist influence.

(2) 戒厳令下 *kaigen-rei-ka* "under martial law."

BASE: 戒厳令 *kaigen-rei* "martial law."

戒厳令下の北京は静けさに包まれた。
Kaigen-rei-ka no Pekin wa shizukesa ni tsutsumareta.
Beijing under martial law was enveloped in silence.

(3) 検閲下 *ken'etsu-ka* "under censorship."

BASE: 検閲 *ken'etsu* "censorship."

出版物は今でも厳しい検閲下におかれている。
Shuppan-butsu wa ima de mo kibishii ken'etsu-ka ni okarete iru.
Even now, published material is under strict censorship.

(4) 戦時下 *senji-ka* "during wartime."

BASE: 戦時 *senji* "wartime."

戦時下、日用品はほとんど生産されなかった。
Senji-ka, nichiyō-hin wa hotondo seisan sarenakatta.
During wartime, there was almost no production of daily
  necessities.

(5) 新憲法下 *shin-kenpō-ka* "under the new constitution."

BASE: 新憲法 *shin-kenpō* "new constitution."

新憲法下では、女性も選挙権を持っている。
Shin-kenpō-ka de wa, josei mo senkyo-ken o motte iru.
Under the new constitution, women too have the right to vote.

監督 *kantoku* "supervision."	田中政権 *Tanaka-seiken* "the Tanaka administration."
監督下 *kantoku-ka* "under supervision."	田中政権下 *Tanaka-seiken-ka* "under the Tanaka administration."
支配 *shihai* "control, rule."	
支配下 *shihai-ka* "under the control."	占領 *senryō* "occupation."
	占領下 *senryō-ka* "under occupation."

KA

Approximate English Equivalents:
person, expert, -er, -ist.

A word formed with *-ka* denotes a person of a type
specified by the base. In some cases, it is a person with
high social status or with some kind of special knowledge or
skill (examples 5, 6, 7, 8, 9). In other cases, it is a person

with an enthusiasm or disposition of some kind (examples 1, 2, 3, 4, 10). It is generally clear from the meaning of the base which of these two interpretations of *-ka* is involved. In range of use, *-ka* overlaps with several other elements, including 一員 *-in* (q.v.), 一者 *-sha* (q.v.), 一士 *-shi* (q.v.), and 一通 *-tsū* (not included). In many cases, there is a clear contrast when *-ka* occurs with the same base as *-in* or *-sha*. Compare 銀行家 *ginkō-ka* (banker) with 銀行員 *ginkō-in* (bank employee), and 登山家 *tozan-ka* ([expert] mountain climber) with 登山者 *tozan-sha* (person climbing a mountain). In other cases, however, this sort of clear contrast is lacking: 投資家 *tōshi-ka* / 投資者 *tōshi-sha* (investor). For discussion, see Sugimura (1986). It appears that *-ka* is added only to bases of Chinese origin.

Accent: unaccented.

(1) 愛好家 *aikō-ka* "devotee."

BASE: 愛好 *aikō* "being fond."

父は釣りの愛好家として有名だった。

Chichi wa tsuri no aikō-ka toshite yūmei datta.

My father was well-known as a fishing buff.

(2) 勉強家 *benkyō-ka* "studious person."

BASE: 勉強 *benkyō* "studying."

長男は大変な勉強家だ。

Chōnan wa taihen na benkyō-ka da.

The oldest son is a very studious person.

(3) 道徳家 *dōtoku-ka* "moral person."

BASE: 道徳 *dōtoku* "morality."

彼は時代遅れの道徳家だ。

Kare wa jidai-okure no dōtoku-ka da.

He is an old-time moralist.

(4) 活動家 *katsudō-ka* "activist."

BASE: 活動 *katsudō* "activity."

6人の活動家が日本大使館に逃げ込んだ。

Roku-nin no katsudō-ka ga Nihon-taishikan ni nigekonda.

Six activists fled into the Japanese embassy.

(5) 漫画家 *manga-ka* "cartoonist."

BASE: 漫画 *manga* "cartoon."

漫画家は若い人に人気がある。
Manga-ka wa wakai hito ni ninki ga aru.
Cartoonists are popular with young people.

(6) 作曲家 *sakkyoku-ka* "composer."

BASE: 作曲 *sakkyoku* "composing music."

ソ連の作曲家ではショスタコービッチが有名だ。
Soren no sakkyoku-ka de wa Shosutakōbitchi ga yūmei da.
Among Soviet composers, Shostakovich is famous.

(7) 歴史家 *rekishi-ka* "historian."

BASE: 歴史 *rekishi* "history."

あの歴史家は大学で教えながら、歴史小説も書いている。
Ano rekishi-ka wa daigaku de oshienagara, rekishi-shōsetsu mo kaite iru.
That historian is teaching at a university and at the same time writing historical novels.

(8) 専門家 *senmon-ka* "specialist."

BASE: 専門 *senmon* "specialty."

指紋はあの男のものだと専門家が言った。
Shimon wa ano otoko no mono da to senmon-ka ga itta.
A specialist said that the fingerprints were that man's.

(9) 投資家 *tōshi-ka* "investor."

BASE: 投資 *tōshi* "investing."

このごろ投資家は慎重になっている。
Konogoro tōshi-ka wa shinchō ni natte iru.
Investors are cautious these days.

(10) 野心家 *yashin-ka* "ambitious person."

BASE: 野心 *yashin* "ambition."

新しい検事は野心家だといわれている。
Atarashii kenji wa yashin-ka da to iwarete iru.
The new prosecutor is said to be an ambitious person.

冒険 *bōken* "adventure."	小説 *shōsetsu* "novel."	
冒険家 *bōken-ka* "adventurer."	小説家 *shōsetsu-ka* "novelist."	

理論　*riron* "theory."

理論家　*riron-ka* "theoretician."

努力　*doryoku* "effort, exertion."

努力家　*doryoku-ka* "hard worker."

KA

Approximate English Equivalents:
-ization, -ification.

A word formed with *-ka* is a noun denoting a process of change. The change involves turning into or becoming more like what is denoted by the base. A word formed with *-ka* can combine with *suru* to form a verb, and in most cases the verb can be used either transitively or intransitively (Martin 1975: 878). When the verb is used transitively, the subject brings about a change in the direct object (examples 2, 5, 8, 9). When the verb is used intransitively, the subject undergoes a change (examples 1, 3, 4, 10).

Accent: unaccented.

(1) ドーナツ化 *dōnatsu-ka* "becoming donut-like."

BASE: ドーナツ *dōnatsu* "donut."

アメリカの大都市は、中心部に住む人が少なくなって、ドーナツ化してしまっている。

Amerika no dai-toshi wa, chūshin-bu ni sumu hito ga sukunaku natte, dōnatsu-ka shite shimatte iru.

Big cities in the United States, with fewer people living in the central areas, have become (hollowed out) like donuts.

(2) 映画化 *eiga-ka* "making into a movie."

BASE: 映画 *eiga* "movie."

あの小説を映画化することにした。

Ano shōsetsu o eiga-ka suru koto ni shita.

They decided to make that novel into a movie.

(3) 一般化 *ippan-ka* "becoming general."

BASE: 一般 *ippan (no)* "general, common."

日本では核家族が一般化してきた。

Nihon de wa kaku-kazoku ga ippan-ka shite kita.

In Japan, the nuclear family has become general.

(4) 活発化 *kappatsu-ka* "becoming active."

BASE: 活発 *kappatsu (na)* "active."

最近、消費者運動が活発化してきた。
Saikin, shōhi-sha-undō ga kappatsu-ka shite kita.
Recently, the consumer movement has become active.

(5) 記号化 *kigō-ka* "symbolization."

BASE: 記号 *kigō* "symbol."

メタンガスはＣＨ₄と記号化できる。
Metan-gasu wa shī-etchi-fō to kigō-ka dekiru.
You can symbolize methane as CH_4.

(6) 高齢化 *kōrei-ka* "becoming elderly."

BASE: 高齢 *kōrei* "advanced age."

日本の社会は高齢化が進みだした。
Nihon no shakai wa kōrei-ka ga susumidashita.
Japanese society has begun to age.

(7) 温暖化 *ondan-ka* "warming."

BASE: 温暖 *ondan (na)* "warm."

地球の温暖化が問題になってきた。
Chikyū no ondan-ka ga mondai ni natte kita.
Global warming has become an issue.

(8) 製品化 *seihin-ka* "making into a product."

BASE: 製品 *seihin* "product."

この機械を製品化するのに3年ぐらいかかるだろう。
Kono kikai o seihin-ka suru no ni san-nen gurai kakaru darō.
It'll probably take about three years to put this machine into pro-
   duction.

(9) タブー化 *tabū-ka* "making taboo."

BASE: タブー *tabū* "taboo."

この町は精神病の話をタブー化しているらしい。
Kono machi wa seishin-byō no hanashi o tabū-ka shite iru rashii.
This town seems to have made talk of mental illness a taboo.

(10) 全面化 *zenmen-ka* "becoming full-scale."

BASE: 全面 *zenmen* "whole surface."

戦争が全面化したのは1937年だ。
Sensō ga zenmen-ka shita no wa senkyūhyaku-sanjūnana-nen da.
The war became all-out in 1937.

民主 *minshu*
　　"sovereignty of the people."
民主化 *minshu-ka*
　　"democratization."

深刻 *shinkoku (na)* "serious."
深刻化 *shinkoku-ka*
　　"intensification."

機械 *kikai* "machine."
機械化 *kikai-ka*
　　"mechanization."

近代 *kindai* "modern times."
近代化 *kindai-ka*
　　"modernization."

KAI

Approximate English Equivalents:
meeting, gathering; society, association.

A word formed with *-kai* may denote a meeting or gathering (examples 1, 3, 5), or it may denote an organization that holds meetings (examples 2, 4). The base may specify the activity (examples 1, 2, 3), the participants (example 4), or the occasion (example 5).

Accent: ¬*-kai*.

(1) 演奏会 *ensō-kai* "concert, recital."
BASE: 演奏 *ensō* "musical performance."
今年の演奏会には有名なピアニストが出た。
Kotoshi no ensō-kai ni wa yūmei na pianisuto ga deta.
A famous pianist appeared in this year's concert.

(2) 自治会 *jichi-kai* "student council, self-governing body."
BASE: 自治 *jichi* "self-government."
自治会に参加する学生は少なくなっている。
Jichi-kai ni sanka suru gakusei wa sukunaku natte iru.
Fewer students are participating in the student council.

(3) 競技会 *kyōgi-kai* "athletic meet."
BASE: 競技 *kyōgi* "athletic contest."
来年の競技会は5月に行われる。

Rainen no kyōgi-kai wa go-gatsu ni okonawareru.
Next year's athletic meet will be held in May.

(4) 理事会 *riji-kai* "board of directors."

BASE: 理事 *riji* "director."

社長は引退後、理事会の一員になった。
Shachō wa intai-go, riji-kai no ichi-in ni natta.
The company president became a member of the board of directors after retirement.

(5) 新年会 *shinnen-kai* "New Year's party."

BASE: 新年 *shinnen* "New Year."

部長はかぜのため今年の新年会には出なかった。
Buchō wa kaze no tame kotoshi no shinnen-kai ni wa denakatta.
Because of a cold the department head didn't attend the New Year's party this year.

展示　*tenji* "exhibiting."
展示会　*tenji-kai* "an exhibition."

後援　*kōen* "support."
後援会　*kōen-kai*
"support association, booster's club, election committee."

送別　*sōbetsu* "farewell."
送別会　*sōbetsu-kai* "farewell party."

演説　*enzetsu* "speech."
演説会　*enzetsu-kai* "speech contest."

界
KAI

Approximate English Equivalents: world, circles.

A word formed with *-kai* denotes a sector of society involved in a realm of activity denoted by the base. There are also a number of examples that denote a natural or a religious realm: 動物界 *dōbutsu-kai* (the animal world) and 天上界 *tenjō-kai* (the celestial world).

Accent: ⌐*-kai.*

(1) 芸能界 *geinō-kai* "show business world."

BASE: 芸能 *geinō* "performing arts, show business."

ハリウッドはアメリカの芸能界の中心地だ。

Hariuddo wa Amerika no geinō-kai no chūshin-chi da.
Hollywood is the center of the American show business world.

(2) 実業界 *jitsugyō-kai* "business circles."

BASE: 実業 *jitsugyō* "business."

彼は実業界では有名だ。
Kare wa jitsugyō-kai de wa yūmei da.
He is famous in business circles.

(3) 金融界 *kin'yū-kai* "financial world."

BASE: 金融 *kin'yū* "finance."

彼は金融界の第一人者だ。
Kare wa kin'yū-kai no daiichinin-sha da.
He is the leader of the financial world.

(4) 社交界 *shakō-kai* "society circles."

BASE: 社交 *shakō* "social intercourse."

彼女の離婚は社交界のニュースとなった。
Kanojo no rikon wa shakō-kai no nyūsu to natta.
Her divorce became news in society circles.

(5) スポーツ界 *supōtsu-kai* "sports world."

BASE: スポーツ *supōtsu* "sports."

日本のスポーツ界ではプロ野球選手の地位は特に高い。
*Nihon no supōtsu-kai de wa puro-yakyū-senshu no chii wa toku
   ni takai.*
In the Japanese sports world, the status of professional baseball
   players is especially high.

文学　*bungaku* "literature."
文学界　*bungaku-kai*
　　"the literary world."

経済　*keizai* "economy."
経済界　*keizai-kai*
　　"economic circles."

教育　*kyōiku* "education."
教育界　*kyōiku-kai*
　　"the world of education."

工業　*kōgyō*
　　"industry, manufacturing."
工業界　*kōgyō-kai*
　　"industrial circles."

感
KAN

Approximate English Equivalents:
feeling, sense.

A word formed with *-kan* denotes a sensation or an emotion that involves what is denoted by the base. In most cases, this pattern is used for transitory feelings that arise as responses to immediate circumstances, but there are also words that denote enduring sentiments (examples 3, 7, 8, 9). The range of use of *-kan* thus overlaps with that of 一心 *-shin* (q.v.).

Accent: ⁻*-kan*.

(1) 安定感 *antei-kan* "feeling of stability."

BASE: 安定 *antei* "stability."

この車は古いので、何となく安定感がない。
Kono kuruma wa furui no de, nanto-naku antei-kan ga nai.
This car is old and somehow lacks a sense of stability.

(2) 圧迫感 *appaku-kan* "a feeling of pressure."

BASE: 圧迫 *appaku* "pressure."

オリンピックの選手は精神的圧迫感と闘わなければならない。
Orinpikku no senshu wa seishin-teki appaku-kan to tatakawa-nakereba naranai.
Olympic athletes have to struggle with psychological pressure.

(3) 一体感 *ittai-kan* "sense of unity."

BASE: 一体 *ittai* "one body."

少数民族は強い一体感をもっているようだ。
Shōsū-minzoku wa tsuyoi ittai-kan o motte iru yō da.
Minority groups seem to have a strong sense of unity.

(4) 解放感 *kaihō-kan* "sense of liberation."

BASE: 解放 *kaihō* "liberation."

彼は高校を卒業したとたん大きな解放感を味わった。
Kare wa kōkō o sotsugyō shita totan ōki na kaihō-kan o aji-watta.
No sooner had he graduated from high school than he felt a tremendous sense of liberation.

(5) 空腹感 *kūfuku-kan* "feeling of hunger."

BASE: 空腹 *kūfuku* "hunger."

空腹感のために、仕事に集中できなくなった。

Kūfuku-kan no tame ni, shigoto ni shūchū dekinaku natta.

A feeling of hunger kept me from concentrating on my work.

(6) 恐怖感 *kyōfu-kan* "feeling of fear."

BASE: 恐怖 *kyōfu* "fear."

彼の言葉は国民に恐怖感をあたえた。

Kare no kotoba wa kokumin ni kyōfu-kan o ataeta.

His words threw fear into the people.

(7) 責任感 *sekinin-kan* "sense of responsibility."

BASE: 責任 *sekinin* "responsibility."

彼は責任感の強い若者だ。

Kare wa sekinin-kan no tsuyoi wakamono da.

He is a young man with a strong sense of responsibility.

(8) 使命感 *shimei-kan* "sense of mission."

BASE: 使命 *shimei* "mission."

田中さんは仕事に対して使命感をもっている。

Tanaka-san wa shigoto ni taishite shimei-kan o motte iru.

Tanaka feels a sense of mission toward his work.

(9) 信頼感 *shinrai-kan* "feeling of trust."

BASE: 信頼 *shinrai* "trust."

不景気が続くと、政府への信頼感がなくなるだろう。

Fu-keiki ga tsuzuku to, seifu e no shinrai-kan ga nakunaru darō.

If the economic slump continues, trust in the government will
  probably be lost.

(10) スピード感 *supīdo-kan* "sensation of speed."

BASE: スピード *supīdo* "speed."

ここのジェットコースターのスピード感はすごい。

Koko no jetto-kōsutā no supīdo-kan wa sugoi.

The roller coaster here gives an incredible sensation of speed.

正義 *seigi* "justice."	劣等 *rettō* "inferiority."
正義感 *seigi-kan* "sense of justice."	劣等感 *rettō-kan* "feeling of inferiority."
満足 *manzoku* "satisfaction."	危機 *kiki* "crisis."

満足感	*manzoku-kan*	危機感	*kiki-kan*
	"feeling of satisfaction."		"feeling of crisis."

KAN

Approximate English Equivalent: view.

A word formed with *-kan* denotes a person's outlook or ideas concerning what is denoted by the base. There are also a few examples of a different pattern, in which the word formed with *-kan* denotes a view like what is denoted by the base: 先入観 *sennyū-kan* (preconception), 一面観 *ichimen-kan* (one-sided view).

Accent: ⌐-*kan* (the accent has shifted off the devoiced vowel in example 5: *kachi-kān* 価値観).

(1) アメリカ観 *Amerika-kan* "view of the U.S."

BASE: アメリカ *Amerika* "the U.S."

彼のアメリカ観は正しいと思う。
Kare no Amerika-kan wa tadashii to omou.
I think his view of the United States is correct.

(2) 人生観 *jinsei-kan* "view of life."

BASE: 人生 *jinsei* "life."

結婚したら、人生観は大きく変わってくるだろう。
Kekkon shitara, jinsei-kan wa ōkiku kawatte kuru darō.
When you get married, your view of life will probably change a lot.

(3) 人間観 *ningen-kan* "view of human beings."

BASE: 人間 *ningen* "human being(s)."

私はヒトラーの人間観がわからない。
Watashi wa Hitorā no ningen-kan ga wakaranai.
I don't understand Hitler's view of human beings.

(4) 女性観 *josei-kan* "view of women."

BASE: 女性 *josei* "women."

この本を読んだとき、作者の女性観を疑った。
Kono hon o yonda toki, sakusha no josei-kan o utagatta.
When I read this book, I wondered about the author's view of women.

(5) 価値観 *kachi-kan* "one's values."

BASE: 価値 *kachi* "value."

私たちの価値観はだいぶ違う。
Watashi-tachi no kachi-kan wa daibu chigau.
Our values are quite different.

(6) 結婚観 *kekkon-kan* "view of marriage."

BASE: 結婚 *kekkon* "marriage."

彼の結婚観を知りたい。
Kare no kekkon-kan o shiritai.
I want to know his views on marriage.

(7) 倫理観 *rinri-kan* "ethical views."

BASE: 倫理 *rinri* "ethics."

今回のシンポジウムのテーマは「医者の倫理観」に決まった。
Konkai no shinpojiumu no tēma wa "isha no rinri-kan" ni ki-matta.
It has been decided that the theme of the coming symposium will
  be "The Ethical Views of Doctors."

(8) 死生観 *shisei-kan* "view of life and death."

BASE: 死生 *shisei* "life and death."

あの事件で私の死生観は大きく変わった。
Ano jiken de watashi no shisei-kan wa ōkiku kawatta.
That incident greatly changed my view of life and death.

(9) 天皇観 *tennō-kan* "view of the Emperor."

BASE: 天皇 *tennō* "the Emperor."

ＧＨＱは日本人の天皇観を問題にした。
Jī-etchi-kyū wa Nihon-jin no tennō-kan o mondai ni shita.
The GHQ questioned the Japanese view of the Emperor.

(10) 宇宙観 *uchū-kan* "view of the universe."

BASE: 宇宙 *uchū* "the universe."

今と昔では宇宙観に大きな違いがある。
Ima to mukashi de wa uchū-kan ni ōki na chigai ga aru.
Comparing the present with the past, there is a big difference in
  our view of the universe.

道徳　*dōtoku* "morality."　　　　　自然　*shizen* "nature."

道徳観 *dōtoku-kan* "view of morality."	自然観 *shizen-kan* "view of nature."
世界 *sekai* "world."	歴史 *rekishi* "history."
世界観 *sekai-kan* "world view."	歴史観 *rekishi-kan* "view of history."

KEN

Approximate English Equivalents:
sphere, radius.

In most cases a word formed with *-ken* denotes the range within which what is denoted by the base occurs or is found (examples 1, 2, 4, 5). When the base is the name of a country (example 3), the word with *-ken* denotes that country's sphere of influence. There are also a few examples of a different kind, in which the word formed with *-ken* denotes the area surrounding what is denoted by the base: 首都圏 *shuto-ken* (The National Capital [=Tokyo] Region), 南極圏 *nankyoku-ken* (area below the Antarctic Circle).

Accent: ⌐*-ken*.

(1) 爆撃圏 *bakugeki-ken* "bombing radius."

BASE: 爆撃 *bakugeki* "bombing."

B29の爆撃圏が広くなった。
Bī-nijūku no bakugeki-ken ga hiroku natta.
The bombing range of the B29s was extended.

(2) 仏教圏 *Bukkyō-ken* "the Buddhist sphere."

BASE: 仏教 *Bukkyō* "Buddhism."

日本は6世紀以来仏教圏に入っている。
Nihon wa roku-seiki irai Bukkyō-ken ni haitte iru.
Japan has been in the Buddhist sphere since the sixth century.

(3) ソ連圏 *Soren-ken* "the Soviet Bloc."

BASE: ソ連 *Soren* "Soviet Union."

ソ連圏にはいろいろな民族が生活している。
Soren-ken ni wa iroiro na minzoku ga seikatsu shite iru.
There are many different peoples living in the Soviet Bloc.

(4) 通貨圏 *tsūka-ken* "currency bloc."

BASE: 通貨 *tsūka* "currency."

ドイツ・マルクの通貨圏はこれから広くなるだろう。
Doitsu-maruku no tsūka-ken wa kore kara hiroku naru darō.
The German mark currency bloc will probably grow from here
on.

(5) 通勤圏 *tsūkin-ken* "commuting radius."

BASE: 通勤 *tsūkin* "commuting to work."

鉄道のおかげで東京の通勤圏が拡大した。
Tetsudō no okage de Tōkyō no tsūkin-ken ga kakudai shita.
Thanks to the railroads, Tokyo's commuting radius has grown.

文化 *bunka* "culture."	勢力 *seiryoku* "influence."
文化圏 *bunka-ken* "cultural sphere."	勢力圏 *seiryoku-ken* "sphere of influence."
共産 *kyōsan* "communal ownership."	支配 *shihai* "control."
共産圏 *Kyōsan-ken* "the Communist Bloc."	支配圏 *shihai-ken* "sphere of control."

Approximate English Equivalent:
money.

A word formed with *-kin* denotes money of a kind specified by the base. In range of use, *-kin* overlaps with 一代
-dai (q.v.), 一費 *-hi* (q.v.), and 一料 *-ryō* (q.v.), but its
range is much broader, and words formed with *-kin* do not
necessarily denote payments. For discussion, see Kimura
(1986: 103).

Accent: unaccented (所持金 *shoji-kin* in example 5 is an exception).

(1) 軍用金 *gun'yō-kin* "military funds, war chest."

BASE: 軍用 *gun'yō (no)* "for military use."

軍用金を集めるため、政府は新しく計画を立てている。
*Gun'yō-kin o atsumeru tame, seifu wa atarashiku keikaku o
tatete iru.*

The government is forming a new plan to raise military funds.

(2) 報奨金 *hōshō-kin* "cash bonus, reward money."

BASE: 報奨 *hōshō* "reward."

警察は鈴木さんに報奨金を出すことにした。
Keisatsu wa Suzuki-san ni hōshō-kin o dasu koto ni shita.
The police decided to pay a reward to Suzuki.

(3) 借入金 *kariire-kin* "borrowed money."

BASE: 借り入れ *kariire* "borrowing."

彼は借入金で商売をしている。
Kare wa kariire-kin de shōbai o shite iru.
He is conducting his business with borrowed money.

(4) 入学金 *nyūgaku-kin* "enrollment fee."

BASE: 入学 *nyūgaku* "enrolling."

大学の入学金はとても高い。
Daigaku no nyūgaku-kin wa totemo takai.
University enrollment fees are very high.

(5) 所持金 *shoji-kin* "spending money, money on hand."

BASE: 所持 *shoji* "possessing, carrying."

彼はきのう家にあった所持金10万円を盗まれた。
Kare wa kinō ie ni atta shoji-kin jū-man-en o nusumareta.
Yesterday, the ¥100,000 in spending money he had at home was stolen.

賠償 *baishō* "compensation."	契約 *keiyaku* "contract."
賠償金 *baishō-kin* "reparations."	契約金 *keiyaku-kin* "signing bonus."
補助 *hojo* "aid, assistance."	予備 *yobi* "a reserve."
補助金 *hojo-kin* "subsidy."	予備金 *yobi-kin* "reserve funds."

工
KŌ

Approximate English Equivalent:
worker.

A word formed with *-kō* denotes a worker, typically a factory worker. In some cases, the base specifies the type of work, denoting either the activity itself (examples 1, 4) or an object involved in that activity (example 3). In other cases, the base specifies the worker's status (examples 2, 5). In range of use, *-kō* overlaps with –員 *-in* (q.v.), but *-in* is not limited to words denoting factory workers.

Accent: unaccented.

(1) 印刷工 *insatsu-kō* "press operator."

BASE: 印刷 *insatsu* "printing."

印刷工たちはストをすることに決めた。

Insatsu-kō-tachi wa suto o suru koto ni kimeta.

The press operators decided to go on strike.

(2) 熟練工 *jukuren-kō* "skilled worker."

BASE: 熟練 *jukuren* "skill."

ロボットの導入により熟練工が少なくなった。

Robotto no dōnyū ni yori jukuren-kō ga sukunaku natta.

Due to the introduction of robots, skilled workers have become scarcer.

(3) 機械工 *kikai-kō* "mechanic."

BASE: 機械 *kikai* "machine."

熟練の機械工になるには時間がかかる。

Jukuren no kikai-kō ni naru ni wa jikan ga kakaru.

It takes time to become a skilled mechanic.

(4) 組み立て工 *kumitate-kō* "assembler."

BASE: 組み立て *kumitate* "assembling."

電気器具の組み立て工は女性が多い。

Denki-kigu no kumitate-kō wa josei ga ōi.

Many electric appliance assemblers are women.

(5) 臨時工 *rinji-kō* "temporary worker."

BASE: 臨時 *rinji (no)* "temporary."

この工場には臨時工がたくさんいる。

Kono kōjō ni wa rinji-kō ga takusan iru.

There are many temporary workers at this factory.

配管 *haikan* "plumbing, pipe laying."	訓練 *kunren* "training."
配管工 *haikan-kō* "plumber."	訓練工 *kunren-kō* "trainee worker."

仕上げ　*shiage* "finishing."　　修理　*shūri* "repairing."
仕上げ工　*shiage-kō* "finisher."　　修理工　*shūri-kō* "repairer."

Approximate English Equivalents:
person, -er.

A word formed with *-nin* denotes a person involved in an activity specified by the base. In almost all cases, the person is the agent of the activity; 使用人 *shiyō-nin* (employee) is an exception. The range of *-nin* overlaps with that of 一者 *-sha* (q.v.). Some bases occur with either, and there is no clear difference in meaning in such cases (e.g., 発行人 *hakkō-nin* / 発行者 *hakkō-sha* [publisher]). However, *-sha* is added almost exclusively to bases of Chinese origin, whereas *-nin* occurs freely with native-Japanese bases. Although *-jin* "person, inhabitant" (q.v.) is etymologically related and written with the same *kanji*, it is best thought of as a separate item (Martin 1975: 881).

Accent: unaccented (謀反人 *muhón-nin* in example 7 is an exception).

(1) 傍聴人 *bōchō-nin* "listener."

BASE: 傍聴 *bōchō* "listening."

裁判で傍聴人がメモをとることは許されている。
Saiban de bōchō-nin ga memo o toru koto wa yurusarete iru.
Listeners are allowed to take notes at trials.

(2) 代理人 *dairi-nin* "representative."

BASE: 代理 *dairi* "representation, standing in for."

契約は社長の代理人が行った。
Keiyaku wa shachō no dairi-nin ga okonatta.
The contract was concluded by a representative of the company
　　president.

(3) 発起人 *hokki-nin* "initiator, proposer"

BASE: 発起 *hokki* "initiation, proposal"

有名な科学者が発起人となってこの会が作られた。

89

Yūmei na kagaku-sha ga hokki-nin to natte kono kai ga tsu-kurareta.

This association was formed with a famous scientist as the initiator.

(4) 保証人 *hoshō-nin* "guarantor."

BASE: 保証 *hoshō* "guarantee."

長く滞在する外国人は保証人が必要だ。

Nagaku taizai suru gaikoku-jin wa hoshō-nin ga hitsuyō da.

A foreigner who is going to stay a long time needs a guarantor.

(5) 小作人 *kosaku-nin* "tenant farmer."

BASE: 小作 *kosaku* "tenant farming."

戦後、政府は小作人に土地を売り渡した。

Sengo, seifu wa kosaku-nin ni tochi o uriwatashita.

After the war, the government sold land to tenant farmers.

(6) 見張り人 *mihari-nin* "lookout."

BASE: 見張り *mihari* "keeping watch."

その門のまわりには見張り人がたくさんいた。

Sono mon no mawari ni wa mihari-nin ga takusan ita.

There were many lookouts around that gate.

(7) 謀反人 *muhon-nin* "rebel."

BASE: 謀反 *muhon* "rebellion."

謀反人はみんな島に送られた。

Muhon-nin wa minna shima ni okurareta.

The rebels were all sent to an island.

(8) 料理人 *ryōri-nin* "cook."

BASE: 料理 *ryōri* "cooking, food"

ファミリー・レストランの料理人は学校の先生より給料がいい。

Famirī-resutoran no ryōri-nin wa gakkō no sensei yori kyūryō ga ii.

A cook at a family restaurant makes a better salary than a schoolteacher.

(9) 差出人 *sashidashi-nin* "sender."

BASE: 差し出し *sashidashi* "sending."

差出人の住所・氏名は封筒の左上の隅に書くことになっている。

Sashidashi-nin no jūsho-shimei wa fūtō no hidari-ue no sumi

ni kaku koto ni natte iru.
One is supposed to write the sender's name and address in the upper left-hand corner of the envelope.

(10) 通行人 *tsūkō-nin* "passer-by."

BASE: 通行 *tsūkō* "passing."

その銀行強盗に通行人2人が殺された。
Sono ginkō-gōtō ni tsūkō-nin futari ga korosareta.
Two passers-by were killed by the bank robber.

怪我 *kega* "injury."	勤め *tsutome* "job."
怪我人 *kega-nin* "injured person."	勤め人 *tsutome-nin* "office worker."
見物 *kenbutsu* "sightseeing."	受け取り *uketori* "receiving."
見物人 *kenbutsu-nin* "sightseer."	受取人 *uketori-nin* "recipient."

Approximate English Equivalents:
discussion, debate, opinion, theory.

RON

Words formed with *-ron* fall into a number of different types, but the meaning of *-ron* always involves the notion of a discussion or debate, and in some cases a translation with "discussion" or "debate" is appropriate (examples 4, 9). When the discussion is written (examples 6, 10), *-ron* can often be translated as "essay," "treatise," or "work," whether the work is scholarly or popular. In many cases, a word formed with *-ron* denotes the opinion that someone holds in a debate or controversy (examples 2, 3, 8). The base in a word of this type denotes what is favored or accepted, and it is generally possible to use a corresponding word ending in 派 *-ha* (q.v.) to denote the group of people who hold the opinion in question (e.g., 廃止派 *haishi-ha* "those who favor abolition" corresponds to *haishi-ron* in example 2). This last use of *-ron* overlaps with the range of use of 説 *-setsu* (q.v.). When a discussion or opinion denoted by a word with *-ron* has a scholarly character, a translation with "theory" is often appropriate (examples 1, 5, 7). There are also a few words formed with *-ron* which simply denote a discussion like what is denoted by the base: 抽象論 *chūshō-ron* (abstract argument, generalities).

Accent: ⌐*-ron*.

(1) 文学論 *bungaku-ron* "literary theory."

BASE: 文学 *bungaku* "literature."

彼女の文学論はゲーテの影響を受けている。

Kanojo no bungaku-ron wa Gēte no eikyō o ukete iru.

Her literary theory has been influenced by Goethe.

(2) 廃止論 *haishi-ron* "endorsement of abolition."

BASE: 廃止 *haishi* "abolition."

死刑廃止論は被害者の家族から出た。

Shikei-haishi-ron wa higai-sha no kazoku kara deta.

It was the victim's family that favored abolishing the death penalty.

(3) 北進論 *hokushin-ron* "endorsement of northward expansion."

BASE: 北進 *hokushin* "northward expansion."

軍部は北進論を主張した。

Gunbu wa hokushin-ron o shuchō shita.

The military advocated northward expansion.

(4) 国防論 *kokubō-ron* "debate over national defense."

BASE: 国防 *kokubō* "national defense."

防衛費は今年も国防論の焦点になる。

Bōei-hi wa kotoshi mo kokubō-ron no shōten ni naru.

Defense expenditures will be the focus of the debate over national defense this year too.

(5) 教育論 *kyōiku-ron* "theory of education."

BASE: 教育 *kyōiku* "education."

その大学院生はデューイの教育論に影響された。

Sono daigakuin-sei wa Dyūi no kyōiku-ron ni eikyō sareta.

That graduate student was influenced by Dewey's theory of education.

(6) 『資本論』 *Shihon-ron* "Das Kapital."

BASE: 資本 *shihon* "capital."

『資本論』はマルクスの主著だ。
"Shihon-ron" wa Marukusu no shucho da.
Das Kapital is Marx's principal work.

(7) 進化論 *shinka-ron* "the theory of evolution."

BASE: 進化 *shinka* "evolution."

小学校の教科書にも進化論の説明が出る。
Shōgakkō no kyōkasho ni mo shinka-ron no setsumei ga deru.
Explanations of the theory of evolution appear even in elementary-school textbooks.

(8) 尚早論 *shōsō-ron* "opinion that something is premature."

BASE: 尚早 *shōsō (no)* "premature."

彼は軍備縮小に対して尚早論を主張している。
Kare wa gunbi-shukushō ni taishite shōsō-ron o shuchō shite iru.
In regard to arms reduction, he insists that it is premature.

(9) 体制論 *taisei-ron* "debate over system."

BASE: 体制 *taisei* "system, structure."

国民にとって，体制論より生活の向上の方が大切だった。
Kokumin ni totte, taisei-ron yori seikatsu no kōjō no hō ga taisetsu datta.
For the people, the improvement of their lives was more important than a debate on the political system.

(10) 東京論 *Tōkyō-ron* "discussion of Tokyo."

BASE: 東京 *Tōkyō* "Tokyo."

彼女は都民の生活を中心にした東京論を書いている。
Kanojo wa tomin no seikatsu o chūshin ni shita Tōkyō-ron o kaite iru.
She has written (is writing) a study of Tokyo that focuses on the lives of its citizens.

芸術 *geijutsu* "art."
芸術論 *geijutsu-ron* "discussion of art."

強硬 *kyōkō (na)* "unyielding."
強硬論 *kyōkō-ron* "hard line."

責任 *sekinin* "responsibility."
責任論 *sekinin-ron* "view that someone must take responsibility."

幸福 *kōfuku (na)* "happiness."
幸福論 *kōfuku-ron* "discussion of happiness."

RUI

Approximate English Equivalents:
class, items.

A word formed with *-rui* refers collectively to the members of a class of things specified by the base. When the meaning of the base is broad, all the members of the class fit into the category it denotes (examples 1, 2, 3, 5). When the meaning of the base is narrow, it specifies the class by providing a typical subcategory (example 4).

Accent: ⌐-*rui*.

(1) 道具類 *dōgu-rui* "tools."

BASE: 道具 *dōgu* "tool."

彼の道具類は高い物ばかりだ。
Kare no dōgu-rui wa takai mono bakari da.
His tools are all expensive.

(2) 希ガス類 *kigasu-rui* "the rare gases."

BASE: 希ガス *kigasu* "rare gas."

希ガス類は不活性だ。
Kigasu-rui wa fu-kassei da.
The rare gases are inert.

(3) 昆虫類 *konchū-rui* "the insect class."

BASE: 昆虫 *konchū* "insect."

くもは昆虫類に入らない。
Kumo wa konchū-rui ni hairanai.
Spiders do not belong to the insect class.

(4) オレンジ類 *orenji-rui* "oranges and the like."

BASE: オレンジ *orenji* "orange."

フロリダでは、オレンジ類が値上がりした。
Furorida de wa, orenji-rui ga ne-agari shita.
In Florida, oranges and the like went up in price.

94

(5) 下着類 *shitagi-rui* "underwear items."

BASE: 下着 *shitagi* "underwear."

東京のスーパーには下着類まで揃っている。
Tōkyō no sūpā ni wa shitagi-rui made sorotte iru.
Even underwear items are stocked in Tokyo supermarkets.

ビタミン *bitamin* "vitamin."	野菜 *yasai* "vegetable."
ビタミン類 *bitamin-rui* "vitamins."	野菜類 *yasai-rui* "vegetables."
酒 *sake* "alcoholic beverage."	雑貨 *zakka* "sundries."
酒類 *sake-rui* "liquor."	雑貨類 *zakka-rui* "sundry items."

 力 RYOKU
Approximate English Equivalents:
ability, capacity, power.

A word formed with *-ryoku* denotes the ability or capacity to do or be what is denoted by the base. The range of use of *-ryoku* overlaps with that of 一性 *-sei* (q.v.), and some bases can occur with either (e.g., 生産性 *seisan-sei* [productivity], 生産力 *seisan-ryoku* [productive capacity]), but *-ryoku* is less vague. There are also a few examples of a different pattern, in which the word formed with *-ryoku* denotes a kind of power or strength that comes from what is denoted by the base: 原子力 *genshi-ryoku* (atomic power), 精神力 *seishin-ryoku* (spiritual strength).

Accent: ⁻*-ryoku*.

(1) 爆発力 *bakuhatsu-ryoku* "explosive power."

BASE: 爆発 *bakuhatsu* "explosion."

火薬の爆発力はダイナマイトほどではない。
Kayaku no bakuhatsu-ryoku wa dainamaito hodo de wa nai.
The explosive power of gunpowder is not as great as that of dynamite.

(2) 英語力 *Eigo-ryoku* "English ability."

BASE: 英語 *Eigo* "English."

彼女は英語力に自信がないといった。

Kanojo wa Eigo-ryoku ni jishin ga nai to itta.
She said she has no confidence in her English ability.

(3) 生産力 *seisan-ryoku* "productivity."

BASE: 生産 *seisan* "production."

この新しい工場は旧工場の2倍の生産力がある。
Kono atarashii kōjō wa kyū-kōjō no nibai no seisan-ryoku ga aru.
This new factory has twice the productivity of the old factory.

(4) 破壊力 *hakai-ryoku* "destructive power."

BASE: 破壊 *hakai* "destruction."

去年の台風は恐るべき破壊力を見せた。
Kyonen no taifū wa osorubeki hakai-ryoku o miseta.
Last year's typhoon showed frightening destructive power.

(5) 反撃力 *hangeki-ryoku* "counterattack capability."

BASE: 反撃 *hangeki* "counterattack."

敵は反撃力を増してきた。
Teki wa hangeki-ryoku o mashite kita.
The enemy has built up its counterattack capability.

(6) 記憶力 *kioku-ryoku* "ability to remember."

BASE: 記憶 *kioku* "memory."

年を取ると記憶力が鈍る。
Toshi o toru to kioku-ryoku ga niburu.
As you grow older, your memory weakens.

(7) 耐久力 *taikyū-ryoku* "stamina, durability."

BASE: 耐久 *taikyū* "endurance, durableness."

若い選手は耐久力を養う訓練をしている。
Wakai senshu wa taikyū-ryoku o yashinau kunren o shite iru.
The young players are training to build up stamina.

(8) パンチ力 *panchi-ryoku* "punching power."

BASE: パンチ *panchi* "punch."

フライ級だが、山本選手のパンチ力はすさまじい。
Furai-kyū da ga, Yamamoto-senshu no panchi-ryoku wa susama-jii.
Yamamoto is a flyweight, but he has tremendous punching power.

(9) 説得力 *settoku-ryoku* "persuasive power."

BASE: 説得 *settoku* "persuasion."

彼の話は説得力がない。
Kare no hanashi wa settoku-ryoku ga nai.
What he says is not persuasive.

(10) 抑制力 *yokusei-ryoku* "ability to restrain."

BASE: 抑制 *yokusei* "restraint."

インフレに対して抑制力のある政策が必要だ。
Infure ni taishite yokusei-ryoku no aru seisaku ga hitsuyō da.
A policy capable of controlling inflation is needed.

忍耐　*nintai* "perseverance."　　　　観察　*kansatsu* "observation."
忍耐力　*nintai-ryoku*　　　　　　　観察力　*kansatsu-ryoku*
　　"ability to persevere."　　　　　　　　"powers of observation."

影響　*eikyō* "influence."　　　　　集中　*shūchū* "concentration."
影響力　*eikyō-ryoku*　　　　　　　集中力　*shūchū-ryoku*
　　"power to influence."　　　　　　　　"ability to concentrate."

Approximate English Equivalents:
fee, charge.

A word formed with -*ryō* denotes a fee that must be paid
for what is specified by the base. The base typically denotes an action (examples 1, 3, 4, 5) or clearly implies a
specific action (example 2). It is generally obvious from the
meaning of the base whether the person who performs the
action pays the fee or receives it. In range of use, -*ryō*
overlaps with 一代 -*dai* (q.v.), 一金 -*kin* (q.v.), and 一賃 -*chin*
(not included). For details, see Kimura (1986). Unlike -*dai*,
-*ryō* is generally not used with bases denoting a place to
live or a thing which is actually purchased (Kimura 1986:
99). In addition, bases that denote some kind of manual
labor generally occur with -*dai* or -*chin* rather than -*ryō*
(Kimura 1986: 101). In a few examples, such as 調味料
chōmi-ryō (spices), -*ryō* means something like "ingre-
dient" and is best thought of as a separate item.

Accent: ⌐-*ryō*.

(1) 配達料 *haitatsu-ryō* "delivery charge."

BASE: 配達 *haitatsu* "delivery."

カタログの商品価格は配達料を含んでいる。
Katarogu no shōhin-kakaku wa haitatsu-ryō o fukunde iru.
The price of items in the catalog includes delivery charges.

(2) 保険料 *hoken-ryō* "insurance premium."

BASE: 保険 *hoken* "insurance."

会社は保険料を補助することになった。
Kaisha wa hoken-ryō o hojo suru koto ni natta.
The company will now be subsidizing insurance premiums.

(3) 授業料 *jugyō-ryō* "tuition fee."

BASE: 授業 *jugyō* "instruction, classes."

大学の授業料は去年の1.5倍になった。
Daigaku no jugyō-ryō wa kyonen no ittengo-bai ni natta.
College tuition has increased 1.5 times over last year.

(4) 受信料 *jushin-ryō* "subscription fee."

BASE: 受信 *jushin* "receiving."

ＮＨＫテレビの受信料は3000円に上がった。
Enu-eichi-kē-terebi no jushin-ryō wa sanzen-en ni agatta.
The NHK television subscription fee went up to ¥3,000.

(5) 入場料 *nyūjō-ryō* "admission fee."

BASE: 入場 *nyūjō* "entering a place."

この映画館は学生の入場料が2割引になっている。
Kono eiga-kan wa gakusei no nyūjō-ryō ga ni-waribiki ni natte iru.
At this movie theater, students get a 20% discount on the admission fee.

駐車 *chūsha* "parking."
駐車料 *chūsha-ryō* "parking fee."
出演 *shutsuen* "appearance, performance."
出演料 *shutsuen-ryō* "performance fee."

手数 *tesū* "trouble, inconvenience."
手数料 *tesū-ryō* "service charge."
郵送 *yūsō* "mailing."
郵送料 *yūsō-ryō* "postage."

流
RYŪ

Approximate English Equivalents:
style, -like.

A word formed with *-ryū* means the style or appearance of what is denoted by the the base. According to Bunka-chō (1975: 1096), *-ryū* is a near synonym of 風 *-fū*, but whereas a word with *-fū* tends to be used for the appearance of a person or thing, a word with *-ryū* tends to be used for the way of doing something. The base typically denotes a person (examples 1, 2) or a place (examples 3, 5). There are also many words with *-ryū* that denote traditional artistic schools, as in 観世流 *Kanze-ryū* (the Kanze school of Noh), and in this meaning *-ryū* overlaps with 派 *-ha* (q.v.). Grammatically, a word with *-ryū* can be followed by *no* and used as a noun modifier (examples 2, 5), followed by *ni* and used adverbially (examples 1, 3, 4), or followed by a form of *da* and used as a predicate. (Words denoting traditional schools are exceptional in being free nouns.) There are also examples in which *-ryū* has its literal meaning of "current": 沿岸流 *engan-ryū* (coastal current).

Accent: unaccented.

(1) 自己流 *jiko-ryū (no)* "own personal style."

BASE: 自己 *jiko* "oneself."

書道の先生は自己流に字を書く。

Shodō no sensei wa jiko-ryū ni ji o kaku.

The calligraphy teacher writes characters in his own personal style.

(2) ゴルバチョフ流 *Gorubachofu-ryū (no)* "Gorbachev-style."

BASE: ゴルバチョフ *Gorubachofu* "Gorbachev."

中国はゴルバチョフ流の改革を恐れている。

Chūgoku wa Gorubachofu-ryū no kaikaku o osorete iru.

China fears Gorbachev-style reforms.

(3) 関西流 *Kansai-ryū (no)* "Kansai-style."

BASE: 関西 *Kansai* "the Kansai region."

大阪出身の中原さんは、いつも関西流に「おおきに」と言う。

Ōsaka-shusshin no Nakahara-san wa, itsu mo Kansai-ryū ni "ōki ni" to iu.

Nakahara, who is from Osaka, always says "thank you" [*ōki ni*] in the Kansai style.

(4) 英語流 *Eigo-ryū (no)* "English-like."

BASE: 英語 *Eigo* "the English language."

アメリカ人はフランス語を英語流に発音しがちだ。

Amerika-jin wa Furansu-go o Eigo-ryū ni hatsuon shigachi da.

Americans tend to pronounce French in an English way.

(5) 西欧流 *Seiō-ryū (no)* "Western-European-style."

BASE: 西欧 *Seiō* "Western Europe."

西欧流の産業革命にはいくつかの問題がある。

Seiō-ryū no sangyō-kakumei ni wa ikutsu ka no mondai ga aru.

Industrial revolution in the style of Western Europe presents a number of problems.

川端 *Kawabata* "Kawabata (Yasunari)."	ヨーロッパ *Yōroppa* "Europe."
川端流 *Kawabata-ryū (no)* "Kawabata-style."	ヨーロッパ流 *Yōroppa-ryū (no)* "European-style."
日本人 *Nihon-jin* "Japanese person."	当世 *tōsei* "contemporary (up-to-date) world."
日本人流 *Nihon-jin-ryū (no)* "Japanese-like."	当世流 *tōsei-ryū (no)* "contemporary-style."

生
SEI

Approximate English Equivalents: student, pupil.

A word formed with *-sei* denotes a student or learner of a type specified by the base.

Accent: ⌐*-sei*.

(1) 聴講生 *chōkō-sei* "auditor."

BASE: 聴講 *chōkō* "auditing."

あの教授の講義には聴講生がたくさん出席している。

Ano kyōju no kōgi ni wa chōkō-sei ga takusan shusseki shite iru.
Many auditors are attending that professor's lectures.

(2) 同級生 *dōkyū-sei* "classmate."

BASE: 同級 *dōkyū* "same class."

同級生とのつき合いが学校生活の中心だ。
Dōkyū-sei to no tsukiai ga gakkō-seikatsu no chūshin da.
Associating with classmates is the center of school life.

(3) 研修生 *kenshū-sei* "trainee."

BASE: 研修 *kenshū* "study and training."

今年は約1000人の研修生が日本に来ている。
Kotoshi wa yaku sennin no kenshū-sei ga Nihon ni kite iru.
About 1,000 trainees are in Japan this year.

(4) 卒業生 *sotsugyō-sei* "graduate."

BASE: 卒業 *sotsugyō* "graduation."

我々は一流大学の卒業生しか採らない。
Wareware wa ichiryū-daigaku no sotsugyō-sei shika toranai.
We take only graduates of first-rate universities.

(5) 優等生 *yūtō-sei* "honor student."

BASE: 優等 *yūtō* "excellence."

長男は小学校から高校まで優等生だった。
Chōnan wa shōgakkō kara kōkō made yūtō-sei datta.
The eldest son was an honor student from elementary school through high school.

上級 *jōkyū* "upper level."
上級生 *jōkyū-sei* "upper-level student."

受験 *juken* "taking exams."
受験生 *juken-sei* "student taking exams."

研究 *kenkyū* "research."
研究生 *kenkyū-sei* "research student."

在校 *zaikō* "attendance (at school)."
在校生 *zaikō-sei* "attending (enrolled) student."

性
SEI

Approximate English Equivalents:
-ness, -ity.

A word formed with -*sei* is a noun denoting an attribute specified by the base. The base is often an adjectival noun, but nouns are also possible as bases, provided they can be construed as attributes. In many cases, a word consisting of a noun base followed by -*sei* is related to a word consisting of that same noun base followed by 的 -*teki* (q.v.), as in 生産的 *seisan-teki (na)* (productive) and 生産性 *seisan-sei* (productivity). The sequence -*teki-sei* (as in 生産的性 *seisan-teki-sei*) does not occur. In some cases, the addition of -*sei* to a noun base seems redundant: 自発 *jihatsu* / 自発性 *jihatsu-sei* (spontaneity). In range of use, -*sei* overlaps with 度 -*do* (q.v.) and with 力 -*ryoku* (q.v.), but both these other elements are more specific. There are a few words with -*sei* that cannot function as free nouns (Arakawa 1986: 87). One example is 植物性 *shokubutsu-sei (no)* (vegetable).

Accent: unaccented.

(1) 安全性 *anzen-sei* "safety."

BASE: 安全 *anzen* / ~ *(na)* "safety / safe."

この車の安全性はメーカーが保証している。
Kono kuruma no anzen-sei wa mēkā ga hoshō shite iru.
The manufacturer guarantees the safety of this car.

(2) 独自性 *dokuji-sei* "uniqueness."

BASE: 独自 *dokuji (no)* "unique."

この都市の独自性は、その長い歴史によって保たれている。
Kono toshi no dokuji-sei wa, sono nagai rekishi ni yotte tamotarete iru.
This city's uniqueness is sustained by its long history.

(3) エリート性 *erīto-sei* "eliteness."

BASE: エリート *erīto* "the elite."

まだアイビーリーグ大学にエリート性はあるだろうか。
Mada Aibī-rīgu-daigaku ni erīto-sei wa aru darō ka.

Do the Ivy League universities still retain their eliteness?

(4) 重要性 *jūyō-sei* "importance."

BASE: 重要 *jūyō (na)* "important."

政府はやっと教育の重要性に気がつきだした。
Seifu wa yatto kyōiku no jūyō-sei ni ki ga tsukidashita.
The government has finally begun to recognize the importance of
  education.

(5) 可能性 *kanō-sei* "possibility."

BASE: 可能 *kanō (na)* "possible."

野党が勝つ可能性はとても少ない。
Yatō ga katsu kanō-sei wa totemo sukunai.
The chances of the opposition party's winning are quite small.

(6) 関連性 *kanren-sei* "connection, relevance."

BASE: 関連 *kanren* "link, relation."

弁護士はその証言の関連性を否定した。
Bengo-shi wa sono shōgen no kanren-sei o hitei shita.
The attorney denied the relevance of that testimony.

(7) 国民性 *kokumin-sei* "national character."

BASE: 国民 *kokumin* "the people (of a nation)."

日本の経済力は勤勉な国民性に基づいている。
*Nihon no keizai-ryoku wa kinben na kokumin-sei ni motozuite
  iru.*
Japan's economic power is based on a diligent national character.

(8) 協調性 *kyōchō-sei* "cooperativeness, harmoniousness."

BASE: 協調 *kyōchō* "cooperation, harmony."

オフィスでは協調性が重んじられる。
Ofisu de wa kyōchō-sei ga omonjirareru.
Cooperativeness is valued in the office.

(9) 生産性 *seisan-sei* "productivity."

BASE: 生産 *seisan* "production."

この新しい工場は旧工場よりずっと生産性が高い。
Kono atarashii kōjō wa kyū-kōjō yori zutto seisan-sei ga takai.
Productivity at this new factory is much higher than at the old
  factory.

(10) 多様性 *tayō-sei* "variety."

BASE: 多様 *tayō (na)* "various."

彼女の小説には多様性がある。
Kanojo no shōsetsu ni wa tayō-sei ga aru.
Her novels have variety.

適応 *tekiō* "adaptation."
適応性 *tekiō-sei* "adaptability."

発展 *hatten*
"growth, development."
発展性 *hatten-sei*
"potential for growth
(development)."

感受 *kanju*
"reception of external
stimuli."
感受性 *kanju-sei*
"sensibility, susceptibility."

計画 *keikaku* "plan."
計画性 *keikaku-sei*
"ability to plan, a systematic
nature."

説
SETSU

Approximate English Equivalents:
opinion, theory, doctrine, rumor.

A word formed with *-setsu* denotes an opinion about some
question or issue. This opinion is often a scholarly theory
(examples 1, 3) or a religious doctrine (example 4). In
other cases, the opinion has become a rumor (example 5).
The base may denote the nature of the opinion (examples
2, 3, 4, 5) or the person who proposed it (example 1). The
range of *-setsu* overlaps with that of 論 *-ron* (q.v.), but
-ron does not share the uses illustrated in example 1 (ダー
ウィン論 *Dāuin-ron* means "discussion of Darwin") and
example 5.

Accent: ⌐-setsu.

(1) ダーウィン説 *Dāuin-setsu* "Darwinian theory."

BASE: ダーウィン *Dāuin* "Darwin."

アメリカではダーウィン説を信じないキリスト教徒もいる。
Amerika de wa Dāuin-setsu o shinjinai Kirisuto-kyōto mo iru.
In the United States, there are Christians who do not believe the
Darwinian theory.

(2) 違憲説 *iken-setsu* "opinion that something is unconstitutional."

104

BASE: 違憲 *iken (no)* "unconstitutional."

自衛隊について違憲説をとっている学者もいる。

Jiei-tai ni tsuite iken-setsu o totte iru gakusha mo iru.

Some scholars take the position that the Self-Defense Forces are unconstitutional.

(3) 脳死説 *nōshi-setsu* "brain death theory."

BASE: 脳死 *nōshi* "brain death."

脳死説にはまだ多くの問題が残っている。

Nōshi-setsu ni wa mada ōku no mondai ga nokotte iru.

Many problems still remain concerning the brain death theory.

(4) 輪廻説 *rinne-setsu* "doctrine of transmigration."

BASE: 輪廻 *rinne* "transmigration of souls."

輪廻説は仏教の基本的な教えだ。

Rinne-setsu wa Bukkyō no kihon-teki na oshie da.

The doctrine of transmigration is a fundamental teaching of Buddhism.

(5) 死亡説 *shibō-setsu* "rumor of someone's death."

BASE: 死亡 *shibō* "death."

近ごろ大統領の死亡説が流れている。

Chikagoro daitōryō no shibō-setsu ga nagarete iru.

Lately a rumor of the president's death has been circulating.

波動 *hadō*
"wave motion, undulation."
波動説 *hadō-setsu*
"the wave theory (of light)."

遺伝 *iden* "heredity."
遺伝説 *iden-setsu*
"theory of heredity."

大陸移動 *tairiku-idō*
"continental drift."
大陸移動説 *tairiku-idō-setsu*
"continental drift theory."

自殺 *jisatsu* "suicide."
自殺説 *jisatsu-setsu*
"rumor (or, supposition concerning the possibilities) of someone's suicide."

者
SHA

Approximate English Equivalents:
person, -er, -ee.

A word formed with *-sha* denotes a person of a kind specified by the base. In most cases, the base is an action or activity and the person is the agent, but there are also examples that do not fit this pattern. Some words with *-sha* have a base that denotes an attribute (e.g., 権力者 *kenryoku-sha* [a person of power], 高齢者 *kōrei-sha* [elderly person]). Others have an action base but do not denote the agent (e.g., 容疑者 *yōgi-sha* [suspect] in example 10 and 逮捕者 *taiho-sha* [person under arrest]). For discussion, see Sugimura (1986: 92–93). In range of use, *-sha* overlaps with a number of other elements, including 一員 *-in* (q.v.), 一家 *-ka* (q.v.), and 一士 *-shi* (q.v.). The nearest synonym is 一人 *-nin* (q.v.), but unlike *-nin*, *-sha* occurs almost exclusively with bases of Chinese origin. One of the rare exceptions is 引き揚げ者 *hikiage-sha* (evacuee).

Accent: ⌐*-sha*.

(1) 視聴者 *shichō-sha* "viewer, listener."

BASE: 視聴 *shichō* "looking and listening."

視聴者の葉書を読むテレビ番組に人気が集まってきた。

Shichō-sha no hagaki o yomu terebi-bangumi ni ninki ga atsu-matte kita.

Television programs on which postcards from viewers are read have become popular.

(2) 常習者 *jōshū-sha* "habitual user."

BASE: 常習 *jōshū* "habitual use."

麻薬の常習者が毎年増えている。

Mayaku no jōshū-sha ga mainen fuete iru.

Drug addicts are increasing every year.

(3) 重傷者 *jūshō-sha* "seriously injured person."

BASE: 重傷 *jūshō* "serious injury."

この事故で重傷者が3人出た。

Kono jiko de jūshō-sha ga sannin deta.

Three people were seriously injured in this accident.

(4) 教育者 *kyōiku-sha* "educator."

BASE: 教育 *kyōiku* "education."

来年のシンポジウムにはソ連の教育者も参加する。

Rainen no shinpojiumu ni wa Soren no kyōiku-sha mo sanka suru.

Educators from the Soviet Union will also participate in next
year's symposium.

(5) 密航者 *mikkō-sha* "stowaway."

BASE: 密航 *mikkō* "stowing away."

密航者は夜になると甲板に出た。
Mikkō-sha wa yoru ni naru to kanpan ni deta.
The stowaway came out on deck at night.

(6) 納税者 *nōzei-sha* "taxpayer."

BASE: 納税 *nōzei* "paying taxes."

税務署の前に納税者の長い列ができた。
Zeimu-sho no mae ni nōzei-sha no nagai retsu ga dekita.
A long line of taxpayers formed in front of the tax office.

(7) 主唱者 *shushō-sha* "advocate."

BASE: 主唱 *shushō* "advocating."

彼らは軍縮の主唱者となった。
Karera wa gunshuku no shushō-sha to natta.
They became advocates of arms reduction.

(8) 遭難者 *sōnan-sha* "disaster victim."

BASE: 遭難 *sōnan* "accident, disaster."

遭難者の帽子は雪の上にあった。
Sōnan-sha no bōshi wa yuki no ue ni atta.
The victim's hat lay on the snow.

(9) 創始者 *sōshi-sha* "originator."

BASE: 創始 *sōshi* "origination."

グーテンベルクは活版印刷術の創始者だった。
Gūtenberuku wa kappan-insatsu-jutsu no sōshi-sha datta.
Gutenberg was the originator of the movable-type printing tech-
nique.

(10) 容疑者 *yōgi-sha* "suspect."

BASE: 容疑 *yōgi* "suspicion."

容疑者はまもなく逮捕された。
Yōgi-sha wa mamonaku taiho sareta.
The suspect was soon arrested.

独裁 *dokusai* "dictatorship."
独裁者 *dokusai-sha* "dictator."

戦死 *senshi* "death in war."
戦死者 *senshi-sha* "one killed in war."

権力 *kenryoku* "power."
権力者 *kenryoku-sha* "person in power."

高齢 *kōrei* "advanced age."
高齢者 *kōrei-sha* "elderly person."

Approximate English Equivalents: practitioner, -er.

SHI

A word formed with *-shi* denotes a person who does a job that requires special knowledge or skill. In some cases, a word with *-shi* implies a license of some kind (e.g., 建築士 *kenchiku-shi* [licensed architect]; cf. 建築家 *kenchiku-ka* [architect]). The base typically denotes the activity involved in the job (examples 1, 3, 5), but there are also cases in which it denotes the area of expertise (examples 2, 4). Several other elements are commonly used in words denoting persons performing jobs: −員 *-in* (q.v.), −工 *-kō* (q.v.), −人 *-nin* (q.v.), −者 *-sha* (q.v.), −師 *-shi* (q.v.), −手 *-shu* (not included). Words with −士 *-shi* differ in that they are terms of respect, and it is not uncommon to see *-shi* used in place of one of these other elements to provide an honorific nuance: 調理士 *chōri-shi* (cook; cf. 調理人 *chōri-nin*), 整備士 *seibi-shi* (maintenance worker; cf. 整備工 *seibi-kō* / 整備員 *seibi-in*), 運転士 *unten-shi* (driver; cf. 運転手 *unten-shu*). When −家 *-ka* (q.v.) is used to mean "expert" it has a similar respectful nuance and is a near synonym of *-shi*; some bases occur with both: 飛行家 *hikō-ka* / 飛行士 *hikō-shi* (flyer). There are also examples with *-shi* that denote holders of academic degrees: 理学士 *rigaku-shi* (Bachelor of Science).

Accent: ˥-*shi*.

(1) 弁護士 *bengo-shi* "attorney."
BASE: 弁護 *bengo* "(legal) defense."

108

日本は弁護士の数が少ない。
Nihon wa bengo-shi no kazu ga sukunai.
In Japan the number of attorneys is small.

(2) 栄養士 *eiyō-shi* "dietitian."

BASE: 栄養 *eiyō* "nutrition."

次女は病院で栄養士をしている。
Jijo wa byōin de eiyō-shi o shite iru.
The second daughter is working as a dietitian at a hospital.

(3) 会計士 *kaikei-shi* "accountant."

BASE: 会計 *kaikei* "accounting."

彼はやっと会計士の試験にパスした。
Kare wa yatto kaikei-shi no shiken ni pasu shita.
He finally passed the test to become an accountant.

(4) 機関士 *kikan-shi* "locomotive engineer."

BASE: 機関 *kikan* "engine, organization, institution."

鉄道機関士の社会的地位はかなり高かった。
Tetsudō-kikan-shi no shakai-teki-chii wa kanari takakatta.
The social status of railroad engineers was quite high.

(5) 操縦士 *sōjū-shi* "pilot."

BASE: 操縦 *sōjū* "operation, steering."

ジャンボ機はベテラン操縦士のおかげで無事に着陸した。
*Janbo-ki wa beteran-sōjū-shi no okage de buji ni chakuriku
    shita.*
Thanks to the veteran pilot, the jumbo jet landed safely.

調理 *chōri* "cooking."	航海 *kōkai*
調理士 *chōri-shi* "cook, chef."	"sailing, traffic by ship."
	航海士 *kōkai-shi* "ship's mate."
飛行 *hikō* "flying."	
飛行士 *hikō-shi* "flier, pilot."	整備 *seibi* "maintenance."
	整備士 *seibi-shi*
	"maintenance worker."

師
SHI

Approximate English Equivalents:
practitioner, -er.

A word formed with -*shi* denotes a person whose work or activities require special knowledge or skill. In range of use, -*shi* overlaps with 士 -*shi* (q.v.), but 師 -*shi* lacks the honorific nuance. In fact, many words with 師 -*shi* denote a person whose activities are undesirable or illegal (example 3). The base typically denotes the activity itself (examples 1, 2, 3, 4), but it may also denote something involved in the activity (example 5). The element -*shi* is also used as a title for religious leaders: ホメイニ師 *Homeini-shi* (Ayatollah Khomeini); 山中師 *Yamanaka-shi* (Rev. Yamanaka).

Accent: ⌐-*shi*.

(1) 調教師 *chōkyō-shi* "trainer."

BASE: 調教 *chōkyō* "(animal) training."

ライオンはおとなしく調教師の指示に従った。
Raion wa otonashiku chōkyō-shi no shiji ni shitagatta.
The lion meekly obeyed the trainer's commands.

(2) マッサージ師 *massāji-shi* "masseur."

BASE: マッサージ *massāji* "massage."

ヨーロッパではスカンジナビアのマッサージ師がいいという。
Yōroppa de wa Sukanjinabia no massāji-shi ga ii to iu.
In Europe, Scandinavian masseuers are said to be good.

(3) 詐欺師 *sagi-shi* "swindler."

BASE: 詐欺 *sagi* "swindling."

その詐欺師はやっと逮捕された。
Sono sagi-shi wa yatto taiho sareta.
The swindler was finally arrested.

(4) 手品師 *tejina-shi* "magician."

BASE: 手品 *tejina* "slight of hand, magic trick."

手品師は公園で芸を見せた。
Tejina-shi wa kōen de gei o miseta.

A magician displayed his tricks in the park.

(5) 薬剤師 *yakuzai-shi* "pharmacist, druggist."

BASE: 薬剤 *yakuzai* "pharmaceutical, drug."

薬剤師になるためには、免許を取らなければならない。
Yakuzai-shi ni naru tame ni wa, menkyo o toranakereba naranai.
To become a pharmacist, one must obtain a license.

調律 *chōritsu* "tuning (a musical instrument)."		宣教 *senkyō* "missionary work."	
調律師 *chōritsu-shi* "tuner (of musical instruments)."		宣教師 *senkyō-shi* "missionary."	
美容 *biyō* "physical beauty."		理容 *riyō* "haircutting, hairdressing."	
美容師 *biyō-shi* "beautician."		理容師 *riyō-shi* "barber, hairdresser."	

 視 SHI

Approximate English Equivalents:
seeing as, regarding as.

A word formed with *-shi* denotes the action of regarding something to be what is denoted by the base. A word formed with *-shi* can combine with *suru* to form a transitive verb (examples 1–5) meaning "to regard" the direct object in the relevant way (Martin 1975: 878–879). There are also examples of a different kind, in which the base specifies the manner in which someone views something: 客観視 *kyakkan-shi* (viewing objectively), 過大視 *kadai-shi* (attaching too much importance).

Accent: ⌐*-shi*.

(1) 同一視 *dōitsu-shi* "regarding as the same."

BASE: 同一 *dōitsu (no)* "same."

カナダ人はアメリカ人と同一視されることがある。
Kanada-jin wa Amerika-jin to dōitsu-shi sareru koto ga aru.
Canadians are sometimes regarded as the same as Americans.

(2) 異端視 *itan-shi* "regarding as heresy."

BASE: 異端 *itan* "heresy."

その学者の思想はローマ法王から異端視された。
Sono gakusha no shisō wa Rōma-Hōō kara itan-shi sareta.
That scholar's ideas were regarded as heresy by the Pope.

(3) 重大視 *jūdai-shi* "regarding as serious."

BASE: 重大 *jūdai (na)* "serious."

大統領は教育を重大視している。
Daitōryō wa kyōiku o jūdai-shi shite iru.
The President is giving serious regard to education.

(4) スパイ視 *supai-shi* "regarding as a spy."

BASE: スパイ *supai* "spy."

警察は大学生をスパイ視する傾向があった。
Keisatsu wa daigaku-sei o supai-shi suru keikō ga atta.
The police had a tendency to regard college students as spies.

(5) 絶対視 *zettai-shi* "regarding as absolute."

BASE: 絶対 *zettai (no)* "absolute."

彼女は自分の価値観を絶対視している。
Kanojo wa jibun no kachi-kan o zettai-shi shite iru.
She regards her own values as absolute.

疑問 *gimon* "doubt."	危険 *kiken* / ~ *(na)* "danger(ous)."
疑問視 *gimon-shi* "regarding as doubtful."	危険視 *kiken-shi* "regarding as dangerous."
楽観 *rakkan* "optimism."	
楽観視 *rakkan-shi* "regarding optimistically."	問題 *mondai* "problem, issue."
	問題視 *mondai-shi* "regarding as a problem."

式
SHIKI

Approximate English Equivalents:
-style, -type.

A word formed with *-shiki* denotes a type or style specified by the base. In most cases, a word with *-shiki* is followed by *no* and used as a noun modifier (example 4), followed by *ni* and used adverbially (example 1), or followed by a form of *da* and used as a predicate (examples 2, 3). It is possible, however, to use a word with *-shiki* as a free noun (example 5). In range of use, -*shiki* overlaps with 一風 -*fū* (q.v.), 一流 -*ryū* (q.v.), and 一調 -*chō* (q.v.). According to Arakawa (1986: 89), a word with -*shiki* means a type or style that is genuinely or unequivocally like what is denoted by the base, whereas a word with -*fū* means only the feeling or air of what is denoted by the base. In terms of this distinction, -*ryū* and -*chō* seem to be closer to -*fū*. The range of use of -*shiki* also overlaps with that of 一的 -*teki* (q.v.), but a resemblance specified by a word with -*teki* can be either genuine or apparent. Like -*fū* and -*ryū*, -*shiki* is often added to bases denoting organizations (example 1) or places (example 2), but -*shiki* also occurs frequently with bases denoting actions (examples 4, 5). On the other hand, -*shiki* is not added to bases denoting individuals, whereas -*fū* and -*ryū* frequently are. Although 一式 -*shiki* (ceremony), as in 卒業式 *sotsugyō-shiki* (graduation ceremony), and 一式 -*shiki* (formula), as in 化学式 *kagaku-shiki* (chemical formula), are etymologically related and written with the same *kanji*, they are best thought of as separate items.

Accent: unaccented.

(1) 軍隊式 *guntai-shiki* "military style."

BASE: 軍隊 *guntai* "the armed forces."

訓練は軍隊式に行われていた。
Kunren wa guntai-shiki ni okonawarete ita.
The training was carried out military-fashion.

(2) 中国式 *Chūgoku-shiki* "Chinese style."

BASE: 中国 *Chūgoku* "China"

この寺は中国式だといわれている。
Kono tera wa Chūgoku-shiki da to iwarete iru.
This temple is said to be in the Chinese style.

(3) スライド式 *suraido-shiki* "sliding type."

BASE: スライド *suraido* "sliding."

この図書館の書棚はスライド式だ。
Kono tosho-kan no shodana wa suraido-shiki da.
This library's bookshelves are of the sliding type.

(4) 折り畳み式 *oritatami-shiki* "folding type."

BASE: 折り畳み *oritatami* "folding."

折り畳み式の傘は便利だが、あまり丈夫ではない。

Oritatami-shiki no kasa wa benri da ga, amari jōbu de wa nai.

Folding-type umbrellas are convenient, but not very sturdy.

(5) スプレー式 *supurē-shiki* "spray type."

BASE: スプレー *supurē* "spray."

香水の売り上げは好調だが、スプレー式は人気が落ちてきた。

Kōsui no uriage wa kōchō da ga, supurē-shiki wa ninki ga ochite kita.

Perfume sales are strong, but the spray type has lost popularity.

アメリカ *Amerika* "United States."	連発 *renpatsu* "rapid firing."
アメリカ式 *Amerika-shiki* "American type."	連発式 *renpatsu-shiki* "rapid-fire type."
空冷 *kūrei* "air cooling."	組み立て *kumitate* "assembling."
空冷式 *kūrei-shiki* "air-cooled type."	組み立て式 *kumitate-shiki* "assembly type."

心 SHIN

Approximate English Equivalents: spirit, sentiment.

A word formed with -*shin* denotes a psychological characteristic relating to what is denoted by the base. Although words formed with -*shin* are not used to denote transitory feelings that arise in response to immediate circumstances, the range of -*shin* nevertheless overlaps with that of 感 -*kan* (q.v.).

Accent: ⌐-*shin* (the accent has shifted off the devoiced vowel in example 7: *kōtŏku-shin* 公徳心).

(1) 冒険心 *bōken-shin* "spirit of adventure."

BASE: 冒険 *bōken* "adventure."

我々の先祖は冒険心に富んでいた。

Wareware no senzo wa bōken-shin ni tonde ita.

Our ancestors were filled with the spirit of adventure.

(2) 忠誠心 *chūsei-shin* "spirit of loyalty."

BASE: 忠誠 *chūsei* "loyalty."

新しい社員に忠誠心を教え込むことが大事だ。
Atarashii shain ni chūsei-shin o oshiekomu koto ga daiji da.
It is important to instill a spirit of loyalty into new employees.

(3) 反発心 *hanpatsu-shin* "spirit of rebellion."

BASE: 反発 *hanpatsu* "rebelling."

彼は政府に強い反発心をもっていた。
Kare wa seifu ni tsuyoi hanpatsu-shin o motte ita.
His mind was strongly set against the government.

(4) 依頼心 *irai-shin* "tendency to rely on others."

BASE: 依頼 *irai* "reliance."

ここの学生は依頼心が強いので、一人で研究することができない。
Koko no gakusei wa irai-shin ga tsuyoi no de, hitori de kenkyū suru koto ga dekinai.
The students here have a strong tendency to rely on others, and can't do research on their own.

(5) 警戒心 *keikai-shin* "wariness."

BASE: 警戒 *keikai* "caution."

今度の事件は欧米の警戒心を高めるだろう。
Kondo no jiken wa Ōbei no keikai-shin o takameru darō.
The present incident will probably heighten European and American wariness.

(6) 克己心 *kokki-shin* "spirit of self-denial."

BASE: 克己 *kokki* "self-denial."

強い克己心がないと、禅寺での生活は無理だ。
Tsuyoi kokki-shin ga nai to, Zen-dera de no seikatsu wa muri da.
Without a strong spirit of self-denial, life at a Zen temple is impossible.

(7) 公徳心 *kōtoku-shin* "public spirit."

BASE: 公徳 *kōtoku* "public morals."

公園の美しさを保つには人々の公徳心が必要だ。
Kōen no utsukushisa o tamotsu ni wa hitobito no kōtoku-shin ga hitsuyō da.

To maintain the beauty of our parks, people must be public spirited.

(8) 利己心 *riko-shin* "selfishness."

BASE: 利己 *riko* "self-interest."

「手伝いたくない」といって息子は利己心をむき出しにした。

"Tetsudaitaku nai" to itte musuko wa riko-shin o mukidashi ni shita.

The son revealed his selfishness by saying, "I don't want to help."

(9) 対抗心 *taikō-shin* "feelings of rivalry."

BASE: 対抗 *taikō* "rivalry."

彼には父親への対抗心がある。

Kare ni wa chichi-oya e no taikō-shin ga aru.

He has feelings of rivalry toward his father.

(10) 闘争心 *tōsō-shin* "combativeness."

BASE: 闘争 *tōsō* "battle, struggle."

彼女の闘争心は失敗のショックから生まれた。

Kanojo no tōsō-shin wa shippai no shokku kara umareta.

Her combative spirit came from the shock of failure.

愛国 *aikoku* "love of country."	慈悲 *jihi* "mercy."
愛国心 *aikoku-shin* "patriotic spirit."	慈悲心 *jihi-shin* "merciful spirit."
競争 *kyōsō* "competition."	虚栄 *kyoei* "vanity."
競争心 *kyōsō-shin* "competitive spirit."	虚栄心 *kyoei-shin* "vain spirit."

層
SŌ

Approximate English Equivalents:
class, stratum.

A word formed with -*sō* denotes a stratum or subgroup of a society or of some large organization. The base may specify the kind of people who are members (examples 1, 3, 7, 8), the kind of criterion used to determine membership (example 6), or something the members have in common (examples 2, 4, 5, 9, 10). When what the members have in common is an opinion or idea (examples 5, 10), -*sō* can be replaced with 一派 -*ha* (q.v.). There are also many scientific words in which -*sō* has its literal meaning of "layer, stratum": 電離層 *denri-sō* (ionosphere), 石炭層 *sekitan-sō* (coal seam).

Accent: ⌐-*sō*.

(1) 閣僚層 *kakuryō-sō* "cabinet-minister class."

BASE: 閣僚 *kakuryō* "cabinet minister."

そのような考え方は閣僚層に多い。
Sono yō na kangaekata wa kakuryō-sō ni ōi.
That kind of thinking is common in the cabinet-minister class.

(2) 知識層 *chishiki-sō* "intelligentsia."

BASE: 知識 *chishiki* "knowledge."

マルクス主義は知識層に広まった。
Marukusu-shugi wa chishiki-sō ni hiromatta.
Marxism spread to the intelligentsia.

(3) 読者層 *dokusha-sō* "class of readers."

BASE: 読者 *dokusha* "reader."

この漫画は読者層が広い。
Kono manga wa dokusha-sō ga hiroi.
This comic has a broad class of readers.

(4) 若年層 *jakunen-sō* "the younger generation."

BASE: 若年 *jakunen* "youth."

この新しい商品は若年層に人気がある。
Kono atarashii shōhin wa jakunen-sō ni ninki ga aru.

117

This new product is popular among the younger generation.

(5) 無関心層 *mu-kanshin-sō* "those who are indifferent."

BASE: 無関心 *mu-kanshin* "indifference."

労働組合に関しては、若い人の間に無関心層が広がっている。

Rōdō-kumiai ni kanshite wa, wakai hito no aida ni mu-kanshin-sō ga hirogatte iru.

Among young people, the segment indifferent to trade unions is growing.

(6) 年齢層 *nenrei-sō* "age bracket."

BASE: 年齢 *nenrei* "age."

年齢層によって結婚観が違う。

Nenrei-sō ni yotte kekkon-kan ga chigau.

Views on marriage differ according to age bracket.

(7) 農民層 *nōmin-sō* "farming segment."

BASE: 農民 *nōmin* "farmer."

土地問題では農民層にも不満が広がった。

Tochi-mondai de wa nōmin-sō ni mo fuman ga hirogatta.

Dissatisfaction over the land issue also spread among the farming segment.

(8) サラリーマン層 *sararīman-sō* "salaried class."

BASE: サラリーマン *sararīman* "salaried worker."

減税論はサラリーマン層から出てきた。

Genzei-ron wa sararīman-sō kara dete kita.

The argument for a tax reduction came from the salaried class.

(9) 支配層 *shihai-sō* "ruling class."

BASE: 支配 *shihai* "ruling."

支配層の狙いはだれにもわからなかった。

Shihai-sō no nerai wa dare ni mo wakaranakatta.

No one understood the aims of the ruling class.

(10) 支持層 *shiji-sō* "those who support."

BASE: 支持 *shiji* "support."

社会党の支持層には女性が多かった。

Shakai-tō no shiji-sō ni wa josei ga ōkatta.

There were many women among the supporters of the Socialist Party.

学生	*gakusei* "student."	指導	*shidō* "leading."
学生層	*gakusei-sō* "student class."	指導層	*shidō-sō* "leader class."
観客	*kankyaku* "spectator."	主婦	*shufu* "housewife."
観客層	*kankyaku-sō* "class of audience."	主婦層	*shufu-sō* "housewife segment."

TAI

Approximate English Equivalents:
group, corps.

A word formed with *-tai* denotes a group of people organized to accomplish some purpose. The group is typically military or quasi-military, although the range of use of *-tai* overlaps with that of 団 *-dan* (q.v.). It also overlaps with 班 *-han* (not included), but *-han* is limited to relatively small groups. In most cases, the base of a word with *-tai* denotes the purpose of the group, although there are also examples in which the base denotes the kind of person in the group (example 2). Occasionally, a word with *-tai* denotes a group consisting of something other than people: トラック隊 *torakku-tai* (truck convoy).

Accent: unaccented.

(1) デモ隊 *demo-tai* "group of demonstrators."

BASE: デモ *demo* "demonstration."

デモ隊の指導者は60歳の男だった。
Demo-tai no shidō-sha wa rokujussai no otoko datta.
The leader of the demonstrators was a 60-year-old man.

(2) 警官隊 *keikan-tai* "police force."

BASE: 警官 *keikan* "police officer."

警官隊を増やすべきだ。
Keikan-tai o fuyasu beki da.
The police force should be strengthened.

(3) 先発隊 *senpatsu-tai* "advance party."

BASE: 先発 *senpatsu* "going in advance."

先発隊の責任はとても重い。
Senpatsu-tai no sekinin wa totemo omoi.
The responsibilities of the advance party are very heavy.

(4) 救助隊 *kyūjo-tai* "rescue party."

BASE: 救助 *kyūjo* "rescue."

登山者は救助隊によって助けられた。
Tozan-sha wa kyūjo-tai ni yotte tasukerareta.
The mountain climber was saved by a rescue party.

(5) パトロール隊 *patorōru-tai* "patrol."

BASE: パトロール *patorōru* "patrolling."

彼はスキー場パトロール隊に入った。
Kare wa sukī-jō-patorōru-tai ni haitta.
He joined the ski patrol.

(6) 軍楽隊 *gungaku-tai* "military band."

BASE: 軍楽 *gungaku* "military music"

兵士とともに軍楽隊がパレードした。
Heishi to tomo ni gungaku-tai ga parēdo shita.
A military band paraded along with the soldiers.

(7) 合唱隊 *gasshō-tai* "a chorus."

BASE: 合唱 *gasshō* "choral singing."

合唱隊はバスで放送局へ向かった。
Gasshō-tai wa basu de hōsōkyoku e mukatta.
The chorus left for the broadcasting station in a bus.

(8) 消防隊 *shōbō-tai* "fire company."

BASE: 消防 *shōbō* "fire fighting."

新しい消防隊は先週から訓練を始めた。
Atarashii shōbō-tai wa senshū kara kunren o hajimeta.
The new fire company began training last week.

(9) 捜査隊 *sōsa-tai* "investigation team."

BASE: 捜査 *sōsa* "investigation."

捜査隊はまだ証拠を集めている。
Sōsa-tai wa mada shōko o atsumete iru.
The investigation team is still gathering evidence.

(10) 探検隊 *tanken-tai* "exploration party."

BASE: 探検 *tanken* "exploration."

探検隊は毎年アフリカへ出かける。

Tanken-tai wa mainen Afurika e dekakeru.

An exploration party sets out for Africa every year.

自衛　*jiei* "self-defense."

自衛隊　*Jiei-tai*
　"the Self-Defense Forces."

音楽　*ongaku* "music."

音楽隊　*ongaku-tai* "band."

航空　*kōkū* "aviation."

航空隊　*kōkū-tai* "air corps."

登山　*tozan*
　"mountain climbing."

登山隊　*tozan-tai*
　"mountain climbing party."

的
TEKI

Approximate English Equivalents:
-like, -ish, -ic, -ive, -al.

A word formed with *-teki* is an adjectival noun denoting an attribute specified by the base. Meiji-period intellectuals chose *-teki* for use in translating new vocabulary from Western languages. The choice was based partly on the meaning of the cognate Chinese element and partly on the resemblance in form to the "-tic" ending of English words like "systematic" and "dramatic" (Umegaki 1975: 151; Hara 1986: 73). At first, words with *-teki* were followed by *no* when used as noun modifiers (Hara 1986: 74), and even today it is not uncommon to find *no* instead of *na* in written Japanese (Martin 1975: 763), but this complication is ignored in the examples below. Depending on the meaning of the base and the context, a word with *-teki* can mean "like," "based on, in accord with," or simply "pertaining to, involving" what is denoted by the base (Hara 1986: 73). For the most part, *-teki* is not added to bases which are (or can be) adjectival nouns, but there are a few exceptions (Hara 1986: 75). In range, *-teki* overlaps with several more specific elements, including 風 *-fū* (q.v.) and 式 *-shiki* (q.v.). For most words with *-teki*, there is a corresponding word with 性 *-sei* (q.v.) which denotes the attribute involved as a noun. In addition, words with *-teki* can serve as bases for the negative element 非 *hi-* (q.v.).

Accent: unaccented.

(1) アクロバット的 *akurobatto-teki (na)* "acrobatic."

BASE: アクロバット *akurobatto* "acrobat."

フィギュアスケートはアクロバット的なところがある。

Figyua-sukēto wa akurobatto-teki na tokoro ga aru.

Figure skating has an acrobatic aspect.

(2) 同情的 *dōjō-teki (na)* "sympathetic."

BASE: 同情 *dōjō* "sympathy."

医者は彼女の話を同情的な気持ちで聞いていた。

Isha wa kanojo no hanashi o dōjō-teki na kimochi de kiite ita.

The doctor listened with sympathetic feelings to what she said.

(3) 科学的 *kagaku-teki (na)* "scientific."

BASE: 科学 *kagaku* "science."

科学的な説明としては物足りなかった。

Kagaku-teki na setsumei toshite wa monotarinakatta.

It was lacking as a scientific explanation.

(4) 協力的 *kyōryoku-teki (na)* "cooperative."

BASE: 協力 *kyōryoku* "cooperation."

今年会社に新しく入った若者たちは非常に協力的だ。

Kotoshi kaisha ni atarashiku haitta wakamono-tachi wa hijō ni kyōryoku-teki da.

The young people who joined the company this year are extremely cooperative.

(5) 基本的 *kihon-teki (na)* "basic."

BASE: 基本 *kihon* "basis."

教科書は基本的な知識を伝えるものだ。

Kyōka-sho wa kihon-teki na chishiki o tsutaeru mono da.

Textbooks transmit basic knowledge.

(6) 音楽的 *ongaku-teki (na)* "musical."

BASE: 音楽 *ongaku* "music."

彼の娘も音楽的な才能がある。

Kare no musume mo ongaku-teki na sainō ga aru.

His daughter has musical talent too.

(7) 殺人的 *satsujin-teki (na)* "murderous."

BASE: 殺人 *satsujin* "murder."

野球部は3月から殺人的な訓練を受けている。
Yakyū-bu wa san-gatsu kara satsujin-teki na kunren o ukete iru.
The baseball team has been undergoing murderous training since
  March.

(8) 生理的 *seiri-teki (na)* "physiological."

BASE: 生理 *seiri* "physiology."

男女を生理的な違いによって差別してはいけない。
Danjo o seiri-teki na chigai ni yotte sabetsu shite wa ikenai.
You shouldn't discriminate against men and women according to
  physiological differences.

(9) 世界的 *sekai-teki (na)* "global."

BASE: 世界 *sekai* "world."

公害は世界的な問題になっている。
Kōgai wa sekai-teki na mondai ni natte iru.
Pollution has become a global problem.

(10) 天才的 *tensai-teki (na)* "genius-like."

BASE: 天才 *tensai* "genius."

彼女の子供はしばしば天才的なところがある。
Kanojo no kodomo wa shibashiba tensai-teki na tokoro ga aru.
Her child frequently shows traces of genius.

文化 *bunka* "culture."	社会 *shakai* "society."
文化的 *bunka-teki (na)* "cultural."	社会的 *shakai-teki (na)* "social."
伝統 *dentō* "tradition."	効果 *kōka* "effect."
伝統的 *dentō-teki (na)* "traditional."	効果的 *kōka-teki (na)* "effective."

用
YŌ

Approximate English Equivalents:
use, for.

A word formed with -*yō* means "for use," where the use is
specified by the base. The base may specify intended users
(examples 1, 2, 4) or intended purpose. Purpose may be

specified by a base that denotes an activity (examples 3, 5, 7, 9, 10) or a thing involved in some activity (examples 6, 8). Words with -yō are commonly followed by *no* and used as noun modifiers (examples 1–4, 6–8, 10), but they can also be followed by a form of *da* and used as predicates (example 5).

Accent: unaccented.

(1) 外人用 *gaijin-yō (no)* "for foreigners."

BASE: 外人 *gaijin* "foreigner."

外人用のアパートは驚くほど高い。
Gaijin-yō no apāto wa odoroku hodo takai.
Apartments for foreigners are ridiculously expensive.

(2) 左利き用 *hidarikiki-yō (no)* "for left-handers."

BASE: 左利き *hidarikiki* "left-hander."

プロショップでは左利き用のクラブも売っている。
Puro-shoppu de wa hidarikiki-yō no kurabu mo utte iru.
Pro shops sell left-handed clubs too.

(3) 医療用 *iryō-yō (no)* "for medical use."

BASE: 医療 *iryō* "medical care."

この老人ホームには医療用の電動ベッドもある。
Kono rōjin-hōmu ni wa iryō-yō no dendō-beddo mo aru.
This old people's home even has motorized hospital beds.

(4) 女性用 *josei-yō (no)* "for women."

BASE: 女性 *josei* "woman."

女性用の名刺は少し小さくできている。
Josei-yō no meishi wa sukoshi chiisaku dekite iru.
Name cards for women are made a little smaller.

(5) 携帯用 *keitai-yō (no)* "portable."

BASE: 携帯 *keitai* "carrying along."

私のワープロは携帯用だ。
Watashi no wāpuro wa keitai-yō da.
My word processor is a portable.

(6) 紅茶用 *kōcha-yō (no)* "for black tea."

BASE: 紅茶 *kōcha* "black tea."

彼はいつも紅茶用のポットを机の上に置いている。
Kare wa itsu mo kōcha-yō no potto o tsukue no ue ni oite iru.
He always keeps a pot for making black tea on his desk.

(7) 工事用 *kōji-yō (no)* "for construction."

BASE: 工事 *kōji* "construction."

この道路は工事用の車がたくさん通る。
Kono dōro wa kōji-yō no kuruma ga takusan tōru.
A lot of vehicles involved in construction work pass along this
  street.

(8) パソコン用 *pasokon-yō (no)* "for personal computers."

BASE: パソコン *pasokon* "personal computer."

ソファーの下にパソコン用のフロッピー・ディスクが落ちてい
た。
Sofā no shita ni pasokon-yō no furoppī-disuku ga ochite ita.
A floppy disk for a personal computer had fallen under the sofa.

(9) 料理用 *ryōri-yō (no)* "for cooking."

BASE: 料理 *ryōri* "cooking."

料理用ワインは酸っぱくて、あまりおいしくない。
Ryōri-yō-wain wa suppakute, amari oishiku nai.
Cooking wine is sour and doesn't taste very good.

(10) 装飾用 *sōshoku-yō (no)* "decorative."

BASE: 装飾 *sōshoku* "decoration."

装飾用のカレンダーをプレゼントする人が増えている。
Sōshoku-yō no karendā o purezento suru hito ga fuete iru.
The number of people who make presents of decorative calen-
  dars has increased.

外出 *gaishutsu* "going out."	家庭 *katei* "household."
外出用 *gaishutsu-yō (no)* "for going out."	家庭用 *katei-yō (no)* "for household use."
事務 *jimu* "office work."	実験 *jikken* "experiment."
事務用 *jimu-yō (no)* "for office use."	実験用 *jikken-yō (no)* "for use in experiments."

剤
ZAI

Approximate English Equivalents:
drug, agent.

A word formed with *-zai* denotes a drug (examples 1, 2) or a chemical agent (examples 3, 4, 5) that has the effect denoted by the base. The range of use of *-zai* is essentially identical to that of 薬 *-yaku*, and there are a number of synonymous pairs: 睡眠剤 *suimin-zai* and 睡眠薬 *suimin-yaku* (sleeping drug), and 起爆剤 *kibaku-zai* and 起爆薬 *kibaku-yaku* (priming powder).

Accent: ⌐-*zai*.

(1) 鎮静剤 *chinsei-zai* ''sedative.''

BASE: 鎮静 *chinsei* ''calm.''

眠れないので鎮静剤を飲んだ。
Nemurenai no de chinsei-zai o nonda.
I couldn't sleep, so I took a sedative.

(2) 解熱剤 *genetsu-zai* ''fever medicine.''

BASE: 解熱 *genetsu* ''fever reduction.''

今まで使っていた解熱剤が効かなくなった。
Ima made tsukatte ita genetsu-zai ga kikanaku natta.
The fever medicine I had been using up to now stopped working.

(3) 乾燥剤 *kansō-zai* ''drying agent.''

BASE: 乾燥 *kansō* ''drying.''

カメラバッグの中に乾燥剤を入れた。
Kamera-baggu no naka ni kansō-zai o ireta.
I put a drying agent in the camera bag.

(4) 枯れ葉剤 *kareha-zai* ''defoliant.''

BASE: 枯れ葉 *kareha* ''dead leaf.''

ベトナム戦争では枯れ葉剤が使われた。
Betonamu-sensō de wa kareha-zai ga tsukawareta.
Defoliants were used in the Vietnam War.

(5) 接着剤 *setchaku-zai* ''adhesive agent, glue.''

BASE: 接着 *setchaku* ''adhesion.''

この接着剤は最近発売されたらしい。

Kono setchaku-zai wa saikin hatsubai sareta rashii.

Apparently this glue just recently went on the market.

清涼　*seiryō*
　　　"cooling, refreshing."
清涼剤　*seiryō-zai*
　　　"tonic, restorative."

防臭　*bōshū* "deodorization."
防臭剤　*bōshū-zai*
　"deodorizer, deodorant."

刺激　*shigeki* "stimulation."
刺激剤　*shigeki-zai*
　　　"a stimulant."

消化　*shōka* "digestion."
消化剤　*shōka-zai*
　　　"aid to (drug promoting)
　　　digestion."

Bibliography

Aihara, Shigemori (1986) 相原林司「不— 無— 非— 未—」『日本語学』第 5 巻 3 号 明治書院

Arakawa, Kiyohide (1986) 荒川清秀「—性 —式 —風」『日本語学』第 5 巻 3 号 明治書院

Bunka-chō (1975) 文化庁『外国人のための基本語用例辞典』第 2 版 大蔵省印刷局

Hara, Yukiko (1986) 原 由起子「—的」『日本語学』第 5 巻 3 号 明治書院

Kimura, Hideki (1986) 木村秀樹「—料 —代 —賃 —費 (—金)」『日本語学』第 5 巻 3 号 明治書院

Martin, Samuel E. (1975) *A Reference Grammar of Japanese*. Yale University Press.

Nakagawa, Masayuki (1986) 中川正之「—場 —所」『日本語学』第 5 巻 3 号 明治書院

Sugimura, Hirofumi (1986) 杉村博文「—者 —家」『日本語学』第 5 巻 3 号 明治書院

Umegaki, Minoru (1975) 梅垣 実『日本外来語の研究』第 3 版 研究社

Zimmer, Karl E. (1964) *Affixal Negation in English and Other Languages: An Investigation of Restricted Productivity*. Supplement to *Word*, Monograph No. 5.